Ready 4 Relationship

Ready 4 Relationship

The Self-Growth Guide to Relationship Readiness

A.B. BRACEWELL, MS

ARROWHEART PUBLISHING

Published by ArrowHeart Publishing

ISBN: 978-0-578-73580-1

Book design by Tyora Moody, tywebbincreations.com

Contents

Acknowledgments

I would like to express my gratitude to everyone that has supported me through the creation of this book. To my son Jeovanni Bracewell Blocker, you are the reason why I strive to be a better man. I live to be an example that you can be proud of. I do and will always love you my son.

To all of my friends and family. Brother, sisters, nephews, nieces, aunts, uncles, cousins; you all have played a part in making me the man that I am today, thank you. My church family, I am so grateful for the spiritual guidance that has helped me develop into Christ-like maturity and pushing me recognize my mission in this world, thank you. My childhood friends , adult friends, colleagues, you all have been there to encourage me, support me, uplift me; I am grateful to have you as my village.

To my editor Tanisha Stewart, to my book designer Tywebbin Creations LLC; I thank you for all of the time and energy you dedicated to this project.

A.B. Bracewell, MS

I thank everyone that has liked, loved, comment, and followed me on social media; your feedback gives me the courage to keep pushing. Thank you.

Introduction

How do we know when we are truly ready for a relationship? Is it when we have reached a certain age? Is it when we meet that *special someone*? Is it when we have graduated college, found a good job, gotten our credit score to 800, traveled the world, or bought a house? Does that make us ready? These are the external factors we often use as a measuring stick for relationship readiness. We believe that when our checklist has been marked off and our "to do's" are completed it is time. This might be true for many things in life, but when it comes to relationships, things are never that black and white. We have emotions, memories, habits, and beliefs that affect our relationship readiness. We give all our attention to the *external* checklists, which give us the appearance of having it all together. But we often ignore the *internal* list, our inner being, those parts that really makes us the person we are. Those are the parts that prepare us to be in a long lasting, loving, and healthy relationship.

That internal list is the true indicator of whether we are ready or not. Our emotional health – that is what sustains a relationship through the different terrains that we will eventually travel. Our sense of self is what keeps us strong when times are hard. It is the substance of our spirit that encourages us to keep it together when things seem like they are falling apart. Yes, it is good to be well educated. Having a great credit score is beneficial. Seeing the world is enlightening. But it is our mental maturity, emotional intelligence, and spiritual steadfastness that makes a much bigger difference in our relationships. So I ask again, how do we know when we are ready for a relationship? That is what this book is all about.

Throughout these pages, we will discuss four key areas of self-growth. Four areas that must be developed and strengthened in order to become ready for a healthy blossoming relationship. Before we get into what these four areas are, I will agree that there are many who choose not to focus on these aspects of their lives, yet they are in relationships. I can also say without a shadow of doubt that those relationships are not functioning at their fullest potential.

As previously stated, relationships nor people are black and white. We have a whole lot of gray areas.

We pick up things along the way. We experience things that affect us. We endure moments that take away our innocence. We encounter people that can damage the way we see ourselves, and all of these things can have a negative impact on our self-growth, which hinders us from being ready for a healthy relationship. This is why I believe that it is crucial for us to grow in these areas of life in order to experience the love that we want. I have observed how challenges in these four areas of one's internal self always lead to challenges in a person's external relationships.

Using this as the framework for the work that I do as a clinician with individuals, couples, and families, I have come to the conclusion that these four areas of self-growth are a direct path to relationship readiness.

You might be wondering, what are these four areas? I will no longer leave you in suspense. Through my work, I have discovered that the majority of relational problems stem from a failure to *heal from past hurt, not forming a relationship with God, not knowing who we are as individuals* and *not developing a mutuality mindset.* Although I have written these areas in the form of a list, they affect our lives in no particular steps or order. I do not know where your need is. But what I do know and what I do understand is that when we find ourselves in a continuous struggle of relationship pain, it can be traced back to one of these areas. If we can never find the intimacy and chemistry we yearn for, the problem can usually be found in one or all of these areas of life, and these pages will guide you through your journey to the answers that you seek.

This book is therapy. We will take this journey together as we find self-growth on this path to relationship readiness. You and I will be forced to look in the mirror and address the person that has been holding you back from becoming that person who can look at their reflection and say with confidence, "I am ready!"

Ready for one person might mean that you no longer sabotage relationships. Ready for another person might mean that you no longer take wounds and scars from one relationship to the next. Ready might mean that you will stop measuring your worth by the person that you are with. Ready might mean that you no longer put any relationship with a person before your relationship with God. Or it can mean that you are ready to be vulnerable, open, communicative, accommodating to someone else. These are all roads that you might have to travel. The purpose of this book this book is to give you assurance and comfort in knowing that you never have to walk that road alone again. Are you ready?

1. Healing from Past Hurt

Many of us are unprepared for a relationship because of internal battles. Our pain, hang-ups, and trauma from the past. These experiences are usually the real reason why we avoid relationships, sabotage them, or destroy them when we enter into one. It boils down to a lack of healing. We all have either been through something or we have witnessed something that has affected our perceptions on love and relationships. It has caused us to grow more distrusting, hateful, and resentful toward connecting with people. These past experiences, which gave birth to our pain and brokenness, are one of the biggest reasons why a good relationship seems to be a distant fantasy for so many of us.

Our own thoughts, feelings, and behaviors have

become barriers. We allow those memories to take refuge in our minds. We give our pain power over our hearts. We issue our hurt and fear a permit to control our attitude and perspectives. We grant our wounds the permission to hinder us from finding companionship. This lack of healing stops us from being in the type of relationship that we desire. This hurt and disappointment easily transforms into bitterness, anger, and sadness on the inside of us. We then allow those emotions to take root in our soul. Before we realize it, our bitter and jaded attitudes toward dating, relationships, and love become who the world sees us to be.

We attempt to blame it on the lack of good prospects, social media, and even God at times, when the reality is that our internal issues are getting in the way. It is time to stop pointing the finger at others and heal the pain that lies within ourselves.

In this section, we will explore how important it is to break through those internal walls built out of heartache, broken trust, and abuse. The walls that we have constructed, which block us from being ready for the type of relationship that we were created to be in. We will examine the shields that we believe are protecting us from loving the wrong person, not realizing that they have become a barricade that traps us in and also stops us from giving love to the right person. We will walk through the steps which lead to healing from past hurt.

We will begin the search for internal joy, personal happiness, and the love that is waiting for us on the other side. This journey will be emotionally taxing. It will stab us in places that we have been trying to hide and ignore. When this journey is over, you will discover that wanting a relationship and being ready for a relationship are two different things. We will be confident that we are finally prepared for that person who has been preparing him or herself for us all of this time.

Taking Ownership

Self-accountability might be one of the most difficult processes for us to participate in. Especially when we feel that our hurt and brokenness was caused by someone else's actions. It is extremely hard for us to take the focus away from their wrongdoing, which caused us the pain, and to look at how we contributed to our own heartache. It is a challenge to explore the reasons why we allowed and accepted a certain type of treatment. Looking at why we are repeatedly attracted to the same types of unhealthy individuals takes a lot of labor. Examining the circumstances or the state of mind that we were in which lead us to stay six months, five years, or even ten years with someone that did not treat us in the way that we should have been treated is not an easy task. It is hard because replaying the sequence of events brings up painful memories. It is also hard because after we take ownership of the part that we played, that means that we are responsible for the change that need to take place if we want to heal.

Change is hard. Even when it is a change for the better. If change was easy we could just stop eating sweets and exercise to drop those fifteen pounds. If changing was simple we could simply stop the drug, the porn, or the shopping addictions. If change was effortless we would be able to break the cycle of negative relationships that we find ourselves in time after time. But it is not, and that is why taking ownership is such a challenging but important step. In order to really heal from the past, change negative patterns, and address our insecurities to prepare ourselves for the relationship that we really want and deserve, we must first learn to take ownership of the part that we played in our own pain.

We are never just helpless victims. In order to begin taking ownership over our change we must get into that mind frame. If we remain in the victim role, believing that someone else is totally responsible for our hurt, that also means that we give someone else the power to be totally responsible for our healing. A chronic cheater needs an individual that will stick around long enough to be repeatedly cheated on. A user needs a person that is willing to be taken advantage of over and over again. A liar needs someone that is willing to overlook their red flags and pardon all of their inconsistencies. By no means am I insensitive to the plight of someone that suffers through this mistreatment. I am trying to communicate that staying in a victim role will only ensure that you will be victimized again. This is about taking your power back.

A part of taking ownership is asking ourselves the tough questions: "Was I an enabler?" "Did I ignore the red flags?" "Did I make excuses for my perpetrator?" "Did I try to hide them from being exposed?" "Do I lack the self-esteem and sense of self-worth to feel that I deserved better or could do better?" "What was my role?" Taking ownership will lead to learning the lesson that needs to be learned that will prepare us for tomorrow. It helps us understand how we can do things better the next time we meet someone. This is a necessary step that we need to take in order to move toward healing. Claiming ownership over our contribution forces us to take a deep and long stare at ourselves. It will help us to see our own issues with self. It will uncover why we accepted and exposed ourselves to things that hurt for so long. It will also give us a better understanding of how that hurt is hurting our chances of finding true love.

When we take ownership we might discover that we have a fear of rejection and abandonment, and that is why we accept anything just to feel that we are a part of something. We may learn that we have a scarcity mindset, and that is why we think that there are not enough quality men or women to select from, and we settle for someone that we know is not good for us. We will understand how our feeling of unworthiness makes us hold onto the notion that this person is the best that the world has to offer. Perhaps we will realize that our self-esteem has been so crushed that we feel lucky anyone would bother with us, even if that attention is totally toxic and harmful.

The key is to take ownership of the reason so that we can change and heal from whatever the issues might be. To be ready for a relationship we must be ready to own our shortcomings. We must examine why we expect and accept less than what we have a right and privilege to. You are the perfect person to discover what events have molded your thoughts and feelings. You can receive help in that discovery but no one can do it for you. You must own your process of healing.

Overcoming hurt from the past is a process. It takes time and plenty of effort. It is not a straight road that comes with a sequence of steps that will lead us to healing. It is a bumpy road filled with peaks and valleys. We will experience good days and bad days during the process. There will be times when we feel victorious, then there will be times when we will feel extremely defeated. That is all a part of the journey. Everyone's starting point is different, and everyone's route has its own twists, turns, and straight ways; however, all of those roads should have the same finish line: healing. When we break that tape, we want to cross over into a place of mental, emotional, physical, and spiritual peace.

It is my belief that you are ready for that peace, and you have gotten to the point where you are willing to take ownership and begin your process. The simple fact that you have taken the time to seek knowledge and understanding through this book tells me that you are ready for a new chapter in life. You no longer want to give the power to heal or hurt to someone else. The fact that you are reading this shows that you are ready to begin your journey. You have developed the resilience to make it through the ups and downs, peaks and valleys, twists and turns that come with this migration from hurt to healing. Taking ownership is a huge step in repairing what has been broken in you. It is your time to be empowered. It is time to stop being a passenger in your own life and get in the driver's seat. Control your decision to improve, restore, and get ready for what the future holds. If you are remembering some of the wrong decisions that you have made, if you are thinking about the red flags that you intentionally overlooked, if you are reliving some of the memories of your past, good: that means that you are at the perfect place. You are face to face with the things you once ran away from. You are at a place where blame and excuses are stripped away. You are focused on the things that you can change. You are prepared to do some emotional lifting, some mental stretching, and some psychological sweating that leads to healing, and I am right there with you.

Reflection: Take a moment to think of the role you have played in your hurt. What needs to change? How can you improve in that area? Which parts are you willing to take ownership of? Reflect on it, write it down, pray and meditate. Then take control.

Challenging our Paradigm

Many of us have been poorly educated on the meaning and function of relationships. We have received faulty teaching on their purpose. We have witnessed poor examples of what they should look like. We have been misled on what is most important when it comes to building a healthy relationship with someone else. A great majority of the dysfunction that we go through in our relationships are learned behaviors. They are generational lessons that have been taught and passed down from one person to the next. So many of us seem to be stuck in a cycle of harmful connections because of those counterproductive lessons that have been taught. Those toxic beliefs have grown to be a normal way of thinking and functioning. It's a trauma that often goes unnoticed.

In the clinical world there is something called

"developmental trauma". This level of trauma is different from the typical type that we probably are all familiar with. Those horrific life-changing events like a car accident, war, or natural disaster, which we can isolate and easily identify as the traumatic spark. With developmental trauma, the events are not a one-time rare occurrence. The events are ongoing exposure to dysfunction, horrors, and abnormalities throughout our lives, which get woven into the fabric of our belief system and character, and become normalized.

For example, hearing gunshots in the middle of the night for the first time would startle most people. It would cause the average person to jump out of bed, check around the house, and call the police to come out and investigate. That would be a traumatic event to someone that has never experienced it. On the other hand, for someone that has grown up in an environment where it is common to hear gunshots in the middle of the night, that individual would not lose a wink of sleep. That person has developed a numbness and tolerance to something that the average person would see as traumatic. That is developmental trauma. This is the same effect that relational dysfunction has on individuals who grow up being constantly taught and exposed to it. When sexual harassment is an everyday occurrence, when all of your friends have been touched or looked at in some inappropriate way, when the majority cheats, when the common lesson is not to trust a man, and that all women want to use you for money, or that women are to be used for sex, we develop in the belly of the trauma without realizing how abnormal our beliefs, views, and practices in relationships really are. We develop a negative belief system about relationships that is just as harmful and damaging as experiencing a major hurt or heartbreak. The dangerous thing about developing in these distorted views of relationships is that these beliefs seem to be normal because that is all that we have been shown and experienced throughout our lives. But this is not normal. These generational beliefs are not healthy. This is untreated hurt that we have just learned to live with. So, in order to be ready for a relationship we must also heal from this level of normalized pain and challenge the paradigm.

We are at the point in our lives where we can no longer blame the poor teaching that we have had from our parents, family members, or society. If we are mature enough to realize that wrong teaching will not yield us the results that we desire, then we are mature enough to change those beliefs and re-educate ourselves.

As a man raised in America I can admit that a lot

of the teaching I have received about relationships, dating, and women has its foundation laid in misogyny. Many of the examples, conversations, and glorified behaviors encouraged me to view women as sexual objects. It pushed me to look at relationships as something I take from while giving back as little as possible. Monogamy was literally frowned upon, and the guy who juggled several women at the same time was actually celebrated. So if my goal is to one day be ready for a serious relationship with one woman you can only imagine how the conditioning of those beliefs I received since a child will work against that goal. At what point do I choose to re-educate myself about what it takes to be in a happy and healthy relationship? When do I fight these beliefs? Or do I continue to blame my behaviors on the way I was raised? There has to be a point where we realize that the way we were raised is not getting us to the place that we want to be.

I spoke about the toxic beliefs that molded my approach to relationships. What are yours? What beliefs block you from being ready for the type of relationship you need, want, and warrant? Maybe you were taught that people could not and should not be trusted. Or perhaps you grew up witnessing domestic abuse, so now you believe that violence and control is a normal part of relationships. Perhaps you have learned to use your body to manipulate people into giving you what you want, or you believe that by you making yourself sexually available to them that they will become emotionally available to you. Some have been taught that a focus on things such as money, status, looks, etc. are the priority when finding a mate. The point is, we have had experiences and teachings which have distorted our views on people and relationships, and the time has come to heal from those poisoning beliefs that we have been allowing to control our decisions and actions.

Some use therapy, others go to a spiritual mentor, one might read books on healthy love, and there are those that attend workshops and support groups. There are so many ways to re-educate ourselves and debunk those false beliefs we have. But we must begin to own it and we must stop allowing the negative examples and teachings that we learned back then to control us right now. This is what I mean by fixing our beliefs and challenging our paradigm. A lot of times it is our beliefs that are keeping us in a cycle of anger and pain. It is the ideology that we have about the opposite sex and relationships that holds us in constant loneliness. It is incredibly important that we begin to extract those negative beliefs or at a minimum stop generalizing those beliefs and realize that everyone is not the same. Everyone will not inflict the type of hurt and pain that you experienced with someone else just because they share the same sex, race, or culture. And most importantly, you must learn that you deserve better and that what you have been believing is not normal or healthy. Become ready to fix those damaging beliefs and be on your way to becoming ready for the right relationship to enter into your life.

Again I ask, what are those beliefs? Now is the time to really examine that. Search your family tree of teaching, explore your cultural incorrectness, extract your experiential biases, and honestly determine if they are getting you ready for the positive and healthy relationship that you want to be in. If you discover that those lessons from your past are unhealthy and self-sabotaging to your future this is the time to reprogram your mind, retrain you heart, and reboot those behaviors.

Reflection: Review this section and answer all of the questions for yourself. Search for the root of the beliefs that need to be challenged and changed.

Emotional and Mental Regulation

Learning to regulate our emotions is another important step in healing from past trauma and pain. Emotional regulation is the ability to govern our own feelings. It is having the capability to control the way we express and experience our perceptions. Mental and emotional regulation is having the capacity to see our emotions from the proper perspective and then communicate them in the appropriate manner. For example, after a break up, we may experience a feeling of loneliness and sadness. The individual that has challenges with regulating their emotions will allow those feelings to take over their lives. It will begin to affect their work, their parenting, their interactions with friends and family, and so on. Those emotions would be given the permission to grow and snowball, turning into depression, guilt, and self-condemnation. It can go as far as them having suicidal thoughts. The ability to regulate our emotions is important to being ready for a relationship.

An overwhelming majority of the clients that I see for therapy were not born with a neurological disorder and did not experience some kind of brain injury which caused their thinking, emotions, and behavior to fall out of alignment with their reality. Most of them fell into a state of depression, anxiety, or suffering from the inability to regulate their own thoughts and feelings. As you can see, being able to regulate our emotions and thoughts is not only important for the purpose of being ready for a relationship, but it is also vital if we want to be ready to live everyday life.

This makes me think of a gentleman that I briefly consulted with. He came in at the request of his fiancée, hopefully soon-to-be wife. He recognized that he had issues with controlling his emotions. He would become anxious whenever he felt uncertain about his fiancé's whereabouts. This led him to constantly check on her throughout the day. He would track her every move. He would question her when she was not where she said she would be at the exact time she said that she would be there. His anxiety took a major toll on him, her, and the relationship, and his fiancée was contemplating ending the engagement. Two years ago, the gentleman had lost a girlfriend to a fatal car accident, and he never took the time to heal from that loss. So now, the hurt, fear, and anxiety he feels whenever his current partner's whereabouts are not accounted for feels like control, distrust, and anger to his fiancé. He never learned to regulate his emotions connected to his traumatic experience, and it was destroying a subsequent relationship that he was not ready for.

When we are ready to heal from the past we must be ready to go through this part of our healing process. We must learn to properly control the emotions and feelings that sabotage our relationships. So whether the misery comes from a failed relationship with a lover or a childhood experience from an abusive or neglectful caregiver, it is time to deal with the hurt so it no longer impairs and damages our future relationships.

In the psychology world there is a thing called trauma reminders. A trauma reminder happens when a negative thought and painful emotion is triggered by a stimulus or what some might call a "hot button". A hot button can be anything, from a song, or a place, a person, or even the tone of someone's voice. For example, a firm loud voice can automatically remind a person of an abusive relationship that they were in, which causes them to feel and act as if they were back in that abusive relationship. Creating feelings of fear and anxiety. That person who is not able to control those emotions can easily feel that they are entering into another abusive situation, so in order to protect themselves they run or fight back by accusing the other person of being controlling and abusive. Another example of a hot button could be an unresponsive texter or caller. This can stimulate memories of an infidelity which took place when a previous lover was unresponsive to a text or phone call. The individual will feel like they are reliving the traumatic experience of being cheated on and resort to protective and self-preserving responses, when the reality is that their mate was not cheating but maybe had their phone on the charger in another room.

So the task is to redirect our thoughts when we begin to obsess and meditate on the pain of a past relationship, and not generalize our feelings of fear to everything that faintly reminds us of the hurt that we experienced.

We cannot allow our thoughts to run freely without us putting any limits around where they should and should not go. It is time to take total control over what we dwell on mentally. We have to find a way to block that negative self-talk that is birthed from our past, and divert the negative and untrue beliefs that our experiences have made us assign to the opposite sex, love, dating, or marriage. Those poisonous thoughts can make us believe that marriage is a waste of time because the statistics show that over fifty percent of marriages end in divorce. The truth is, over fifty percent of marriages fail because over fifty percent of couples do marriage wrong. But the reality is that marriage has a one hundred percent chance of success if we do marriage the right way; however, if we allow our thoughts and emotions to control us rather than regulating them we will let those numbers scare us away from commitment and marriage. It's all about perspective.

So how do we begin to take authority over our own thoughts and emotions? First, we must identify what is triggering them. Our feelings can be crafty: if we do not remain aware, it may seem like they have a mind of their own, as if they come out of nowhere. They do what they want to do. But that is not true. All emotions have a trigger. They are sparked by something. In order to find out what specifically triggers the emotion that we are trying to overcome we have to do some self-tracking. We need to recount the events that occurred before we began to feel lonely, sad, or depressed, then we must learn how to create the proper space and atmosphere within ourselves to isolate them and address those feelings that lead us down the road of unhealthy thoughts, self-sabotaging behaviors, and fear responses.

We must substitute those emotions by shifting our minds to positive and appropriate thoughts. In the next section we will continue the discussion of realizing our triggers so that we can better regulate our thoughts and emotions. I implore you to reflect on those pervasive thoughts that paralyze you emotionally and stop you from taking the risk of being in a relationship and falling in love.

Reflection: What emotions come up when you think about love, relationships, dating, or the opposite sex? How do you usually handle those emotions? What would you like to change about the way you regulate your feelings?

Knowing and Understanding Your Triggers

I am often asked, "How does a person know when they are healed from the past?" "How can we be sure?" "What are the indicators that we are ready?" and my answer is usually the same. We really don't know that we have moved past the hurt and pain, until the things that use to trigger that hurt and pain no longer do. So, as scary as it might sound, we often do not truly know until we begin dating again. We don't find out until we take the risk, exposing ourselves to the possibility of falling in love and embracing the chance of getting our hearts broken. That is when we see our own reaction to being confronted by something that triggers our fear, insecurity, or trauma. Now before we can even overcome those triggers we must first be able to identify what those triggers are. Many times we feel like we have moved past a person, put a relationship behind us, or forgotten about a particular a pain, until something surprisingly takes us back to that memory and experience which ignites a level of sadness, anger, or fear so strong one would think that the situation just happened yesterday. This is why knowing and understanding what our triggers are is so important. When we know our triggers, we can distinguish the past from the present and the real from our imagination. Understanding our triggers opens the door to healing and victory against them because they have been identified.

I think back to a past relationship that I was in with a young lady. She and I were watching a movie and we began to playfully wrestle. As we bear hugged, gently hit and tickled each other, I decided to end it with a WWE pin down. The moment I got on top of her for the pin, and she could not move her legs or arms, our play wrestling went dramatically wrong. She began to kick, scream, and swing more forcefully. Her laughter turned into tears, and her bear hugs turned to her aggressively pushing me away. I immediately got up, feeling scared and confused. After I helped her to calm down and ensured her that I was not trying to hurt her, she revealed to me that she was raped in her past, and me being on top of her, and her not being able to move triggered that very moment for her. Needless to say we never play-wrestled again. But this reaction happened about four other times throughout the relationship. Random things that were said or done would trigger her fear and anxiety, which eventually took a major toll on our relationship.

So what are triggers? For those that may not fully understand, triggers are things that elicit one of the three basic emotional responses to threat and danger, our "fight, flight, or freeze" response. Anything can be a trigger: A scent, a song, a place, a situation, an event, a behavior, and of course a person. Triggers are usually referenced when we are speaking about traumatic experiences such as abuse, neglect, accidents, infidelity, or anything that led to a tremendous amount of hurt or fear. Knowing and understanding our triggers is so important, because they can elicit an emotional response long after the event has passed or the person is gone out of our lives. We feel like we are reliving the event. Triggers are warning responses made to protect ourselves from danger and preserve our safety. The drawback is that triggers function off the basis of our emotions. If you know anything about our heart and emotions, you know that they make good servants but they are terrible masters. It's not wise to allow them to take full control of our lives.

We all have triggers to different things, so to say that one should heal or overcome their triggers might be unrealistic. What is most important when it comes to our triggers is that we heal from the paralyzing and damaging effects that they have on our lives and relationships. Triggers usually have this negative impact on us when we do not take the proper time to heal. We suppress or deny our feelings instead of processing and dealing with them. Then we make ourselves believe that the feelings are gone away and that we are now ready for a relationship again. But like any problem we experience in life, it never goes away by ignoring it or running from it. It only lies dormant for a period of time, gathering strength and power, and suddenly it totally disrupts us when we least expect it.

We often attempt to ignore our triggers, sore spots, and warning signs instead of dealing with the source of the problem. We blame others and project our insecurities onto them as opposed to trying understand why it's a sore spot for us. We suppress it instead of bringing it to the surface, but it will always rise to the surface. Whether we choose to intentionally address it or allow some random unrelated situation to wake up the sleeping monster in us and destroy our relationships, it will come to the surface.

An easy way to identify if something is a trigger or sore spot is to track when a simple word or action that's said or done by a person we are dating elicits a reaction (emotionally, mentally, or behaviorally) which is totally out of proportion to what happened. Or when our reaction to what was done feels connected to the memory of what a previous lover did. There are also times when the anger, suspicion, disappointment, or whatever feeling we are experiencing is connected to something much deeper than a past lover, such as a childhood memory. The important thing is to accept that triggers do exist, and know that when the emotions that are connected to the trigger are not dealt with properly, they will end up being displaced, and will always get in the way of us being in the healthiest relationship we can be in.

It is important for us to know and understand our triggers because there is a thin line between intuition and insecurity. We must be able to differentiate when our emotional reaction is a part of our baggage or when it is actually a current warning sign for the person we are dating. Knowing that it is our baggage that is being triggered helps us to resist from transferring those feelings onto an innocent romantic prospect and sabotaging an opportunity for love. Knowing our triggers gives us the chance to isolate our emotions and deal with them in a proper way. Understanding why certain thoughts, feelings, or actions are activated helps us in communicating those sore spots to the individual that we are dating so that they know and understand why we responded in a certain way. Perhaps we can even receive support with overcoming them or at least give them the chance to decide if they are willing to stay with us as we overcome them, or leave because it is too much for them to handle – that's only fair. Relationships are hard enough – why should we make them harder by assigning our feelings of anger, sadness, or disappointment to someone that was not the root cause of what we are feeling, or when their intentions may not have been in any way related to our past experiences?

Knowing and understanding our triggers can be tricky at times, because they don't only cause us to assign negative emotions to a person that might be right for us, but triggers can also make us assign pleasurable feelings to the person that might be wrong for us. Don't be fooled! Some triggers elicit pleasurable emotions and thoughts of an ex but are still harmful, especially when the source of those feelings are connected to an unhealthy place. For example, say that we like to feel protected in a relationship but our only understanding of protection is connected to people that are aggressive, confrontational, and are willing to resort to violence in order to protect. So when we see these characteristics in a person it will trigger a pleasurable feeling, but since the feeling is connected to a negative source, we might end up in a relationship with someone that is not only aggressive in protection but aggressive toward us. Triggers that remind us of pleasurable and desired things that we used to do with a past mate are also dangerous because that might be a sign that we have not totally moved past that relationship, and somewhere deep inside we could be holding on to a hope and dream of being with them. This will always have others question our readiness for a new relationship. In upcoming chapters, we will discuss the importance of "knowing yourself" as we prepare for a relationship, which will not only help with getting us to know our triggers, but also help to conquer them.

Before I conclude this section I think that it is important to discuss the difference between triggers and red flags because it is so easy to get the two things confused. They are actually very different. Understanding the differences can either lead to healing from the past or sabotaging our future. We already defined what a trigger is and how it is connected to past experiences.

Red flags are warning signs that elicit the same fight, flight, or freeze response. The major difference is that these emotional responses have two different sources, but we often treat them as one and the same. Red flags do not come from memories or experiences of our past. Red flags are directly connected to the person that we are currently dating or in a relationship with. Someone that lies to you must be seen as a liar. Someone that treats you in an abusive manner must be seen as an abuser. They do not have to be connected to a past memory or experience to know that their actions are wrong and unhealthy. The problem comes in when we take our baggage, issues, and unhealed hurt and call them red flags instead of triggers. When we take a simple miscommunication or misunderstanding and label the individual a liar, that is where the self-sabotage comes in. That is where the undeserved blame, the over-reactions, the avoidance and withdrawal come in. If we understand the difference from our triggers and red flags, we can communicate to our mate the real source of our response, help them to understand where the fear comes from, and then we have an opportunity to let communication, support, and healing into our relationship. Understand the difference.

Reflection: Take the time to identify your triggers. What are the thoughts, feelings, behaviors, and places, which take you back to that time of pain? What things in your relationships have you labeled as a red flag in someone else, when it is actually a trigger for you?

My Fear of Abandonment

It is not always easy for us to walk away from a person once we have experienced abandonment. It is also true that it is not easy for us to walk toward others if we have experienced abandonment. Walking away from hurt or walking toward love can be scary for someone that suffers from the fear of abandonment. These two walks might seem like they are going in two different directions, but when they get to the end of the road they end up at the same destination. Individuals that have a fear of abandonment respond to relationships in one of two ways: they either form a love addiction where they try cling to any hint of love and affection because they are trying to avoid the feeling of being abandoned, or they reject intimacy, closeness, and vulnerability to avoid the feeling of being abandoned. Two different roads which take us to the same destination of fear.

Are we courageous enough to address our own attachment and abandonment issues? Can we confront our fear of being alone? Are we willing to explore why we avoid closeness and intimacy with others? All of these things have their foundation in attachment and abandonment issues. In order to be ready for a relationship and move toward healing, we need to explore the origins of why we continue to live in this cycle of toxicity and fear.

Living with abandonment issues causes us to make relationship decisions that lead to our own pain and re-traumatization. This can result from the decision to cling to an unhealthy relationship because we want to fill a void and are afraid of being alone, or from the decision to avoid closeness and intimacy because we are afraid of getting hurt. The abandonment from our past must be addressed so it no longer sabotages our opportunity to be loved by those that come into our lives. We must discover the source of the fear which repeatedly causes us to allow anything and anyone into our heart. We must get to the bottom of why we are so guarded against loving the wrong person that it has also caused us to miss out on receiving love from the right person.

When we take a look into that mirror and the

reflection shows we have been a star player in many of the problems which have stopped us from developing healthy relationships, that can be a hard pill to swallow. But be encouraged, because that pill might be the remedy to our feelings of emptiness. It can be the medicine to our fear of intimacy, and it can be the cure that heals the wound of abandonment. For many of us that deal with this issue of attachment and abandonment, looking in one mirror will not be enough because we only see our current reflection looking back at us. We have to look back at our reflections from childhood and examine the attachment and abandonment issues that started with one or both of our parents to find the answers. Many times it is the negative effect of an absent father or the impact of a neglectful mother which causes us to struggle with abandonment and attachment issues in our adult relationships.

Poor attachment is not a surface wound. So jumping into another relationship will only serve as a band aid that masks a much deeper injury. The attempt to fill that hole with a man or woman will never make us whole as a person. The core of most attachment and abandonment problems dates back to our childhood, when there was an unhealthy interruption somewhere in the relationship with our caregivers. It has been demonstrated that this interruption, whether it was a real abandonment or just a perceived feeling of abandonment, has a direct negative effect on how we attach to others as an adult. This disconnect from a caregiver leads us on a search to replace his or her love. It causes us to be desperate for the love that we did not receive from our parent, and it turns our basic need for love to a dangerous neediness for love. If this is the issue, if this is the past pain that you have been wrestling with, it is time take complete authority over it. We can no longer allow it to dominate our thoughts, feelings, and actions. In order to be ready for a relationship we will have to defeat those negative feelings that are attached to those past relationships which make us feel unworthy, unwanted, and undeserving.

Let us briefly look at the different ways poor attachment and/or abandonment by those we love and trust as a child can affect the way we love and trust as an adult:

The absent father. When I say absent, I am not solely referring to a father who was not physically present, though that is a major issue. I am also speaking about the father who was emotionally missing. I am also referring to the father that did not provide adequate acceptance, assurance, or confidence in us which communicates to a child that they belong. This too can lead to the feeling of abandonment.

Our fathers are the first men that we get to know when we enter into this world. Our relationship with him or lack thereof can set the tone for how we will interact with men for the rest of our lives.

For women that experience an absent father, it is important that you take out the time to explore the effects that it has had on you. Some women find themselves in a cycle of relationships with men that are mentally and emotionally unavailable. Others realize that they are in constant search for male acceptance, or have an unrealistic idolized idea of their father that was never there. They measure their expectations of men against this fictitious father, which no man can live up to, so they always have reasons to walk away because no man is good enough. These are all examples of the re-traumatization that I spoke about, but because some women never really learned what fatherly love is supposed to look like or feel like, she ends up experimenting with what she thinks it is supposed to be, but that experiment only causes more damage.

I have seen the effects of an absent father in the lives of young women manifest in so many different ways. She is in constant search for that guidance and acceptance from men, but she often tries to gain it by the use of her sexuality. Her unmet need for love and guidance from her father gets substituted by a man that wants to take advantage of her. He sees her emptiness, he sees her insecurities, and he knows her vulnerability; but because she never learned how to distinguish real love like the love that her father was supposed to show from the imaginary love that she created in her head about men, she falls victim to him, and many imposters just like him during her lifetime. This often develops into a distrust toward all men. She feels that no man can be trusted when the reality is she was never taught how to discern a man's actions and interpret his words from her father. She was left to figure things out on her own, which left a long trail of heartbreak along her path. The biggest challenge is, even though she feels that men cannot be trusted, she never stops looking for that fatherly acceptance in men. So you can only imagine how bringing that way of thinking into every new relationship will sabotage her situation, lead to the repeat of the same story over and over again, and stop her from ever being ready for a true relationship.

Boys that struggle with abandonment issues become men with abandonment issues. He searches for guidance, closeness, and approval from a male father figure that was never there. The fortunate ones might find that from a positive role model such as a football coach, an uncle, or a pastor; a man that helps to guide him in the right way and appropriately navigate through manhood. But far too many find that guidance and acceptance in males that are not equipped to lead because they did not have a father to teach them how to become a man. So he finds acceptance and guidance in people that influence him to take the wrong path and encourage him to make bad decisions that can damage his future. He is led by men who teach him to be a womanizer, men that model how to be criminally aggressive, men that condition him to believe that women are only good for sex. The same men that show him these lessons will also abandon him when the negative consequences of his actions occur, leaving him re-traumatized. The absent father in this boy's life has left him feeling angry over the abandonment. He reacts rebelliously against any authority figure because he never learned how to properly respect the authority of his father. He never observed his father loving, caring, or protecting his mother so there was never an appropriate example for him to follow for his relationships. The chances of him being prepared for a healthy relationship are extremely slim.

In the same way, I have seen how poor attachment

and abandonment by a mother affects people throughout their lifetime and during their relationship journey. Our mothers are our first examples of nurturing; they are models of sacrifice. We learn how to care for others by watching our mothers. We learn to love unconditionally from our mothers. Our first release of the bonding hormone oxytocin is experienced when our mother nurses us from her bosom. Those that never experienced that usually have a hard time trusting and bonding as an adult. They seem emotionally detached from events that would elicit some level of feeling from the average person. Developing close relationships is difficult for them. The unfamiliar occurrence of intimacy can be scary.

Entire books have been written about this. For now I only want to plant the seed that sparks curiosity to explore our own issues with attachment and abandonment. I want to plant the seed that leads to the desire to heal from those issues of the past so that we can become better in our present and fully live for our futures.

This is your time to take these issues head on. Discover why it has always been so hard for you to open up and really let someone into your heart. Find out why the thought of being single scares you to death. Get the answers to why you are so uncomfortable with holding hands, looking others in the eyes, or sharing your feelings. This exploration may reveal why you hold onto individuals that you should have let go of. Our attachment and abandonment issues have stopped us from being in a healthy relationship for far too long. This is our time to stop the issues from stopping us.

Reflection: Are you frightened by the thought of being alone? Does closeness make you uncomfortable? Has anyone every described you as clingy or emotionally unavailable? Examine your past relationships and identify the effects that they have had on your ability to attach to or leave others.

Good Grief

Another important step in the process of healing from past disappointments and brokenness is our ability to practice "good grief". The way we grieve the loss of a relationship and the feelings connected to that loss can be the determining factor in whether we successfully move on to our next chapter of life or if we fall into a state of depression for the next several years. Overcoming past hurt and pain is not easy. During the journey toward healing we will experience a variety of emotions, from sadness and anger to denial and shame. We cannot ignore these feelings, and it is extremely dangerous to try to suppress them, but these are some of the unhealthy ways we sometimes choose to grieve. Other times we may turn to self-harming and risky behaviors such as: alcohol, drugs, promiscuity, or prescription meds, thinking that we can distract ourselves from the hurt. But we can never drink, sex, or party the pain away. So learning how to properly grieve and work through those feelings that are connected to the past are of the utmost importance.

All of the emotions that we will go through: denial, anger, sadness, regret, and fear are all very normal. The importance of having a healthy grieving process is so that we do not get permanently stuck in one particular emotion or state of mind. We want to successfully transition from one stage of grief to the next, until we get to the point where we truly feel safe enough to let someone new into our lives, and we are safe enough to be allowed into someone else's life. The first step to a successful transition from being grief-stricken to being in perfect peace is to accept the fact that we are grieving. We have to acknowledge the pain and hurt, and we have to be honest with ourselves or there is no way that we can fully move past the memory and feelings which hinder us.

After we have acknowledged that we are experiencing grief, we then must understand that this feeling is only temporary and this too shall pass. So instead of denying the feeling, go through the feeling. If you must cry then cry; if you must be alone then be alone; if you feel frustrated then get angry, but only for a moment. Never go so deep or stay so long in any negative feeling that it causes you to start thinking, speaking, or behaving in a way where you become toxic to yourself.

Sadness will be there. It is abnormal for one to state that they are not sad after experiencing any kind of pain connected to a relationship. When we speak about practicing good grief, the aim is to not allow that sadness to graduate to depression, and that depression to promote to delusions, and the delusions to escort you into a state of psychosis. This might seem farfetched to those that are not totally familiar with the clinical workings of the mind and emotions, but I am here to tell you that sadness can lead us down a dangerous rabbit hole if we allow it to take control of our lives. The Bible instructs us to "to take captive every thought to make it obedient to Christ." If we do not capture our thoughts, they will become obedient to despair, hopelessness, and regret, and that is a road that only leads to a cycle that will be extremely hard to break.

In practicing good grief, we also want to learn how to properly work through those feelings of regret and shame. What I have learned is that many people might blame others for their pain outwardly, but if we dive inwardly we will see that those same people are struggling with a lot of self-blame and personal regrets. Their look in the mirror produces self-condemnation instead of enlightenment and encouragement. This is a very unhealthy way to grieve. Turning against ourselves during a time of sadness and pain can have a long lasting effect on our self-respect and self-worth, and we know that having a poor perception of ourselves can lead to so many other risky behaviors and poor decisions when it comes to relationships and life in general.

Are you ready to grieve in the proper way? Are you ready to bury it? It is time to lay that final rose on the coffin, and watch your pain, hurt, sadness, and regret get lowered into the ground. It is a must. If you need help with grieving properly, there's help. Never feel like you have to go through it alone. Good grief is all about experiencing the hurt, being fully human, and then finding a way to move on. Truth be told, the world will keep on spinning, time will keep on ticking, and the person that you are grieving over will keep on living, so why allow sadness and depression to keep your life at a stand-still? There is more happiness to be had, more love to be shared, and more life to be lived. The end of a relationship is not the end of you.

GOOD GRIEF TECHNIQUES

In order to practice good grief, we must learn how to create an atmosphere which puts boundaries around those emotions that turn grieving from healthy to unhealthy. Having the ability to control those feelings that are connected to the past is one of the biggest steps toward moving past the past. In the psychology world, we teach individuals applicable techniques to help them create the space in their lives where emotional and mental regulation are practiced so that good grief is possible. Many of us already do many of the things that I am about to suggest, but what I have discovered is that we do not realize how these things that we do as hobbies and entertainment also have a tremendous healing power over our thoughts and emotions:

DEEP BREATHING

The fact that breathing comes so natural and automatic for some of us we fail to realize how it is also one of the best calming and soothing agents. This is a great technique to use when those emotions begin to affect your anxiety, which makes your thoughts race. Slowly inhaling and exhaling will help you return to a relaxed mental and emotional state. In the book of Genesis, it says that God breathed into man the breath of life, so it makes perfect sense that the when we use the same breath that was given to us, we can breathe new life into a situation that seems to be full of despair.

SOOTHING MUSIC

Music can truly be like therapy to many people. The perfect song can put us in a happy, calming, or peaceful mood. Great lyrics can help us put our feelings into words, and put our thoughts to a smooth melody. Music is not only good for entertainment but it can be one of the best ways to set the atmosphere for peace and serenity. It can turn depression to dance and tears to a foot tap. When trying to heal from the pain of a broken heart, find a good song that helps change the mood, a beat that makes you move, and lyrics that helps you soothe.

MUSCLE MOVEMENT

Yoga, walking, jogging, swimming, etc. are not only good ways to stay physically healthy, but they also help with our mental and emotional health. Besides the scientific connection between exercise and the impact it has on our mood, there are practical ways muscle movements help us to get through our grieving process that are truly beneficial. Combine good music with a good workout and you will find yourself thinking about of plans for your future instead of dwelling on the pain of your past. We can burn off calories instead of sitting at home and burning with anger and resentment. Before you realize it, you would have found a healthy way to go through your grief, and looking good while doing it will be an added benefit.

BIBLE VERSES AND POSITIVE AFFIRMATIONS

Unhealthy grief starts in our minds with the toxic thoughts we entertain and the poisonous memories that we constantly replay in our heads. The best way to combat those negative thoughts is to fight them with positive thoughts, encouraging Bible verses, or empowering affirmations. Auto suggestion is extremely powerful. In my daily life, I use auto suggestion to conquer fear and anxiety. One of my favorite verses is, "God did not give us a spirit of fear, but of power, love, and a sound mind (2 Tim 1:7)." Basic affirmations are also useful and just as powerful. Simply repeating, "I am worthy", "I am beautiful", and "I am blessed" can harness the strength and power we need to defeat those negative thoughts that try to depress us.

PRAYER AND MEDITATION

There may not be a more effective way to create an atmosphere for healing or a better way to journey through the grieving process than through prayer and meditation. Prayer and meditation give us access to a healing power that no amount of music, muscle moment, or deep breathing can bring. Prayer will reveal to you coping skills that you will never find in any psychology book. Prayer is a direct way to communicate with the Creator of it all. We're able to ask for the healing that we seek, and we can be sure that it will be given to us.

Forgive and Let Go

Learning to forgive and let go might be the most important thing that we have to do in order to move past our hurt and pain. We can break up with them, we can divorce them, or we can try to replace them, but none of that matters if we do not learn to forgive and let go of them. Without forgiveness we will never truly be ready for a healthy relationship, because we will never truly be a healthy individual. I once heard it said that "holding onto unforgiveness is like drinking poison and hoping that it kills the other person". The statement illustrates how the toxic effects of holding onto grudges destroys us from the inside and eventually makes its way to the outside of us. It may seem like we are punishing the one that hurt us by being mean toward them, hating them, or talking about them to others, but the reality is that that breeds fear, anger, and resentment and it is all brewing inside of us twenty-four hours a day, seven days a week. So we are really only hurting ourselves.

The fact that you are reading this chapter gives me the sense that you are ready to forgive and let go of the grudges and pain that have been keeping you anchored in a sea bitterness, enmity, and disappointment. It tells me that you are ready to pardon those that hurt and harmed you. Truth be told, that is the only way you will be ready to attract the healthy type of relationships that your heart desires. It is my hope that you are getting to the point where you understand that the unforgiveness, grudges, resentfulness that we hold against others will continue to hold up the blessing that God has for us in a relationship and in life as a whole.

Have you ever tried to date someone that was holding onto a grudge toward an ex mate, a parent, or even a friend? What was that experience like? Did you experience them constantly talking about the wrong that their ex did? Did it feel like the ex was a third person in your relationship – even though they were nowhere around, their influence and presence was constantly felt? Did they project what their ex did to them on to all men or women, and you sensed that they had a disdain toward the opposite sex as a whole? Maybe they seemed more emotionally attached to their pain and suffering than they were emotionally attached to you? Or perhaps you received a lot of unfair blame for their circumstances, sadness, or misery which started to make you feel sad and miserable. Last question: would you say that this person was ready for a relationship?

These are only a few of the possible things that a person might experience when they try to date or enter a relationship without first learning to forgive others. Now let's make it personal. Let's turn the tables on ourselves and stand in the shoes of the unforgiving individual. We must get ready to forgive because we no longer want to be that person who is constantly talking about an ex on a date. We also do not want to be that person who generalizes the opposite sex because we are holding on to resentment and anger toward one member of the group. We must be ready to forgive because we no longer want to be the individual that has grown more comfortable with attaching ourselves to pain than we are comfortable with attaching ourselves to people. This is why we must be ready to practice forgiveness. This is why we must no longer allow the poisonous effects of bitterness and hatred to consume our hearts and minds. You are reading this book because you are ready to stop sabotaging your own life. You would like to right some wrongs or at least let someone that wronged you know that things are alright. You can no longer afford to hold them or yourself prisoner to your pain.

Unforgiveness is a seed that will grow out of control if we do not quickly uproot it. Out of unforgiveness grows hate, prejudices, sorrow, and fear. When we hold onto it we simultaneously are losing ourselves, because those emotions cannot occupy the same space as power, love, and strong mindedness, which is the type of individual that we are created to be. We are never at peace when we are holding onto a grudge. We are uncomfortable in our own skin. Our mood and demeanor are basically controlled by someone else. We are unable to give the best of ourselves to ourselves or to anyone else because we have buried our best under all of the dirt and mess that unforgiveness brings. Besides, what do we plan on doing with the grudge that we carry around? It has absolutely no use or value to us.

The one thing that might be worse than not forgiving others is the destructive practice of not forgiving ourselves. Self-condemnation will always stop us from being ready for a relationship, because we blame ourselves, we beat ourselves up, and we tear ourselves down for things that went wrong in a relationship or things that go wrong in our lives in general. Please do not confuse self-condemnation with taking ownership, because they originate from two totally different places. The inability to forgive ourselves is the birthplace of self-hate, self-doubt, low self-esteem, self-harming, and even suicide. Not forgiving ourselves turns those feelings of resentment, anger, and disappointment inward and causes us to believe that we are unlovable and unworthy. As a result, we begin to look outside of ourselves and outside of God for love and self-worth.

It is my assumption that you are ready to stop blaming yourself, and that is why you are still reading. It is time stop torturing yourself over what went wrong, and it is time to start forgiving. Are you ready to stop putting yourself down? Are you ready to begin believing that you are smart enough, pretty enough, and that you have always been more than worthy?

There is no magic formula or secret steps to forgiving. Forgiving takes two things: First, we must understand that forgiveness is a soul changing experience. It is a spiritual revelation. It is a total character shift. Forgiving is less about what you do and more about who you are. To become a forgiving person, we must be willing to deny our fleshly desire for revenge. We must make the decision to take the high road, and we have to truly believe that we have been forgiven by the Ultimate Forgiver. Secondly, we cannot learn to forgive properly without allowing the Ultimate Forgiver to take control of our hearts. In case you do not know who the Ultimate Forgiver is, I am referring to Jesus. Learning to forgive is not an easy task because it is in our nature to want to remain angry at someone for the wrong that they did to us. It seems totally justifiable to hold someone accountable for our pain, even if that someone is ourselves, or even if it is God. Becoming ready to forgive is a major process in our journey toward healing, and it is something that we will have to do over and over again, whether we are single, engaged, or married. So if you feel that you are now ready for a relationship, you must be the type of person that is ready to forgive and let go.

Reflection: Who do you need to forgive? What do you need to let go of? What do you plan on doing with the grudge that you are carrying around?

Creating Closure

A young lady enters my office for the first time. She looks like she might be in her early thirties. She is well dressed in a designer business suit, perfect posture, and confident. It's my guess that she is an executive wherever she might work. I begin our session with the typical but effective, "So what brings you in today?" She responds with, "I'm not really sure", then goes on to explain the stress that she has been experiencing with a relationship that she has been in for the past five years. She states, "I've been seeing this guy off and on for a few years." The relationship has had way more downs than there have been ups. She caught him cheating at least three times over the past five years, and there have been several other occasions where she has suspected that he was involved with another woman. She explains that there is no trust, poor communication, and that her overall mood fluctuates from sadness, to disappointment, to anger. She explains that she is ready to stop the on-again, off-again merry-go-round that she had been on for the past few years. This last break up he *decided to pack his things and move out of the apartment after a huge argument, while she was at work. She has not heard from him in over a week. He sends her to voicemail, doesn't answer her texts, and has blocked her from his social media. She comes in today confused as to how after five years, he could just walk away without saying a word? She feels depressed and confused because he did not have the maturity or sensitivity to talk to her before he moved out. She wants to move on but feels like she can't until she gets the closure that she needs and deserves.*

If we dare to be honest with ourselves, we just might admit that seeking closure from an ex-lover is often an indirect way of keeping things open. Chasing closure can be the manifestation of our fear of being alone, disguised as a requirement we need in order to move on. It may also be a way to keep the lines of communication open even when we know that we should cut off all contact. As I told the young lady that walked into my office that day, wanting to receive closure from someone else can be a last ditch effort to hold on to a relationship that is over. There are times when we say we want closure but the truth is we are seeking one last chance to state our case, one more opportunity to prove our love. We want to make one more connection, not closure. We waste precious time searching for reasons, explanations, or a grand finale to a relationship when it is clear that it has ended. I understand that when a relationship is over that the mature and proper thing to do is to sit down and have a discussion about the decision to stop dating or stop the relationship. I am not ignoring the fact that it can be totally confusing when a relationship just fades to black, or when they just go "ghost". This is not only puzzling but it can also be damaging to our self-esteem, leaving us wondering, "Is something wrong with me?" We begin to internalize certain thoughts and emotions of inadequacy and deficiency, which lead us to want questions that we are struggling with answered. So we seek closure.

The young lady stated that she was ready to move forward, but with the utmost respect and honesty I told her that she was not. Because in order to move past the memories and emotions of a relationship that has ended, there will be times when we have to learn how to stop looking for closure and learn to create our own closure. We must get to the place where our experience and wisdom concerning that relationship are enough to validate our decision to walk away.

"It is finished" – can there be a more definitive statement? These were the words of Jesus Christ. When it was all over, when all that could be accomplished was accomplished, when the purpose was fulfilled. When this particular season of His journey ended, Jesus' last words were, "It is finished". An important lesson can be learned from those three little words. We must learn that some individuals enter into our lives for a specific reason and season of time. Having the ability to recognize when that reason has been fulfilled and when that season is over is extremely important in creating closure in order to be open to the relationship that we truly need and deserve. We must recognize when a relationship is finished. We often have our futures suspended in time waiting for someone else's words or actions to determine our next move. As we see in the scripture, Jesus determined when it was over. He stated when it was finished, and we possess that same power and strength. He took control of the ending. We do not have to sit and wait for closure. We can create our own closure. Creating our closure is something we must do in order to let go of the past.

Why is so important to create our own closure? It is important because we will never begin the healing process if we do not close the door to who or what has injured us. We will never create the space for a new relationship if we allow an old one to occupy that area of our heart. We will not discover the next chapter in our lives if we do not close our mind, heart, eyes, and emotions on a chapter that we have already been through. Controlling the closure begins with setting boundaries on the things we expose ourselves to. We have to protect ourselves from the things that trigger memories and feelings connected to a relationship which has ended. We must develop the discipline and resistance against traveling down memory lane, because it will only keep us open to the possibility of rekindling a relationship with an ex whose reason and season has passed.

We need to create the mental and emotional space to heal. When we allow someone that has hurt us to continue to walk in and out of our lives, that is similar to leaving an open wound uncovered and expecting it to get better. But the opposite happens: it gets infected, it is exposed to more pain, it gets picked at, and it takes forever to heal. So just like that open wound, if we do not protect our hearts, cover those emotional scars, and securely monitor our minds, it will take us forever to get better and move on. When it eventually heals, the scar tissue around our heart will be so thick it would seem almost impossible to penetrate. We will lose the ability to feel, which will leave us feeling numb and get in the way of being ready for the right relationship when it comes along.

When we are creating closure we must have the discipline to totally cut that individual out of our lives, whether it means permanently or until we have gotten them out of our system and developed the fortitude to not fall back into old habits when temptation and loneliness appear. So yes, we might have to delete phone numbers, set up blocks on our phone and social media, delete our text history, and if our route to work or the supermarket takes you past their home or neighborhood, we might have to find somewhere new to buy groceries. Sometimes it takes extreme measures to create closure, but if you want to move past the emotions and thoughts of an old relationship, this is where it begins. This what I mean by creating the space, having vacancy, so that we are available to new possibilities.

You are preparing to enter a new season of life, and it is time for some spring cleaning. Past hurt, previous pain, and brokenness from former partners are not allowed in your new season. It is time to close the door on what has ended and open the door to new opportunities, new experiences, and a healthier lifestyle, toward a more promising journey. This is the only way that you will truly be ready for a relationship. You can no longer afford to travel around with the same distrust, skepticism, and hurt, taking it from one relationship to the next, thinking that you will get different results. Something old and new cannot occupy the same space. The Bible states that no one can pour new wine into old wine skins. You must totally get rid of the old if you want to nurture and preserve something new. You must create the space for a new love to enter by closing and cutting off the feelings and thoughts connected to whatever or whoever caused the fear and pain in your past. Once you create the space both literally and figuratively, then you can begin on the road toward healing and embark on the journey toward that new love.

The main reason why we must heal from our past hurt in order to be ready for the relationship we are destined to be in, is because those hurts can create demons. What is a demon? Let's define it as an evil or negative spirit, passion, or influence in our lives. When we do not heal, we end up carrying that demon from one relationship to the next relationship. The unhealthy connection to an ex, those triggers, the blaming, that fear of abandonment, and the toxic beliefs that have been passed down. They all come with their own set of demons that will destroy our hope for a healthy relationship. Our hurt affects the way we trust others, it alters the way we communicate, and it hinders our ability to love. . If we happen to suffer from abandonment issues, we can develop that poisonous spirit of being noncommittal.. That's a past demon which needs to be defeated. If we are the one with a toxic belief system about the opposite sex, we could never see a mate as an individual but just as a member of a gender group who is predestined to cheat, nag, lie, etc. That is a judgmental spirit that we will continue to carry.

Each of the above mentioned situations describes a demon that needs to be conquered. All of these hurts fight against God's plan for love, relationships, and marriage. That is why they are demons, and we all have at least one. If you are ready for a real, healthy, edifying relationship then you must be ready to heal. The beauty of it all is that we hold the power within us to conquer anything that is stopping us from being ready for the type of relationship that we desire to be a part of.

In order to release that power, we must start to ask those self-reflecting questions such as: "How did I allow this to happen to me?", "What toxicity did I bring to the relationship?", and "What could I have done differently?" When we begin to take ownership over those things that we can change, that is when we will stop feeling guilty and start seeing the goodness within us. We will stop harboring shame and begin to feel esteemed. We will no longer distrust ourselves but begin to depend on our own ability to make decisions concerning relationships. We will gain confidence in our own competency to judge the character of a potential mate.

There is an Ultimate Healer that we need to be in relationship with who will help us in all other relationships we decide to explore. This relationship does not only heal us in the places we have been wounded, but it also gives us what we need in order to feel whole again. In the next section, we will explore the importance of spirituality as it relates to our relationship readiness. Our spirituality is the foundation of our morals and values. It is the essence of who we were, who we are, and who we will be. If we want to be ready for the relationship that God has prepared for us, then we first must be ready for a relationship with God.

2. Ready for God

This may have been the hardest chapter of the book to write, because one's relationship with God is so personal, and no level of instruction or steps can properly explain how an improved relationship with God will prepare us for better relationships with each other. This is something that we truly have to experience for ourselves in order to get a full understanding. However, let me start by saying this: God loves relationships and He wants relationships for us. After God created the heavens and the earth, the moon and the stars, the animals and Adam, the only thing that He did not like in all of His creation was the fact that man was alone. I say that to help clear our conscience of any beliefs that tell us that our desire to become better prepared for a relationship is somehow against the will of God or unimportant to Him. God loves relationships. I would also like to clear up the purpose of relationships. Many of us believe that relationships are created to bring us joy, love, happiness, and faith; on the contrary, relationships are created for us to be a reflection, an example, and an imitation of God's love, joy, happiness, and faith toward one another. We are made in His image and likeness.

Now that we have cleared that up, let me also say that I am no Bible scholar or theologian. I am simply an imperfect person that totally relies on God's power to do the work in my weakness. If there is any area of my life where I need God's power the most, it would be with dating, love, and relationships. It was not until I decided to form a real relationship with God that I realized how unprepared I was to form a relationship with the woman that He was preparing for me.

As I began to draw closer to God's word and made more of an effort to govern my life according to His will, I began to see the many parallels between what God wants from me in a relationship with Him and things that we all value in a relationship with each other. I began to understand that when the scripture says, "Delight yourself in the Lord, and He will give you the desires of your heart", that it actually meant that He will change the desires of my heart. He changes it from what it used to be before I began to form a relationship with Him to a new set of desires, which are the things that He wants for me. For example, God poured into my heart the desire to be pure as opposed to my desire for lust and lewdness. He began to give my heart the desire to be more open, honest, and transparent in my relationships, as opposed to being manipulative and conniving. He gave me what my heart should desire, as opposed to me making up my own desires and expecting Him to give them to me. Even though God pours these things into our hearts for His glory, there is a huge benefit on our side. The new morals, values, and desires better prepare us for the type of relationship that He would love for us to have with each other.

If I could sum up this entire chapter in one statement, it would be this: "Find it in God and you never have to look for it in man". The peace, joy, identity, love, patience, kindness, acceptance, and intimacy that I longed for from others and sought after in a relationship were fulfilled when I began to develop my relationship with God. Being ready for God actually made me ready to face whatever season of life that I was in, whether it was being single, in a relationship, or even marriage. Do not get me wrong: finding those things in God did not stop me from wanting a relationship with a woman, but it definitely changed my perspective on my role and responsibilities to the person that I would one day be with. My priority is now to be the giver of those things that I once looked to be the

recipient of. Before I decided to build up the spiritual man in me, I approached relationships searching for what I could get, what she could do for me, what she brought to the table, and how can she could complement me. My entire mentality toward relationships was based on receiving because I was attempting to fill voids in my life with a relationship with another person. Before developing a relationship with God, I would use women like bandages. Instead of healing from the hurt and pain, I would just find someone else to cover my wounds to distract myself from my brokenness, a clear indicator that I was not ready for a relationship. Before I decided to get closer to God, I felt that relationships were made to bring me satisfaction, so I would go after women just for the sport and entertainment of it, not necessarily caring about the effects that my actions had on them. I was more focused on getting rid of my boredom, loneliness, or horniness. I was nowhere near ready for a real relationship during those times. I can give several more examples of how not having God as the center of my life had me unprepared to bring someone else into my life. I am also sure that you can give examples of your own experiences and how your attempts to fill certain voids with a man or woman has shaped your thinking and behaviors toward relationships. It is my belief that until you fill those voids with the presence of God as opposed to trying to fill them the presence of the opposite sex, you will never be whole enough or ready enough to be in a healthy relationship with someone else.

By me establishing a stronger faith and warmer connection with God, I learned that my role and responsibility to others is to give. This was a total perspective change when it comes to relationships. I now focus on what I can bring to the table to make a woman's life better. My intentions are focused on what I can give to make her life more peaceful, happier, and loving. By finding those things in my relationship with God, which I once looked for in relationships with people, I have found an unlimited source of joy, love, acceptance, contentment, and peace, so much so that I look to give that to others as the Bible teaches us to do, instead of taking it from others as our flesh teaches us to do. Now, my hope is to share the peace that I find in God as opposed to stealing someone else's peace through hurting and misusing their hearts. My goal in relationships is to be the type of companion that helps provide comfort and acceptance.

Becoming ready for a relationship with God is key

in becoming ready for a relationship with the person that He has for you. When you decide to work on that relationship, you will see how much better you will become as a person. It puts everything and everyone else in its proper perspective. I will be so bold as to say that if you are not ready for a relationship with God you are not ready for any other relationship that He will bring into your life. He brings the peace, love, discipline, contentment, joy, discernment and wisdom that we will need with the one that we will enter into a relationship with.

His Love

Riddle me this: They say that it is better to have found me and lost me than to never have found me at all. What am I? Answer: Love. Love is something that is hard to find. Some spend their entire lives searching for it. So many people would do just about anything to experience it. No matter how many times you have given up on love it never stops you from wanting it. I can confidently say that there is nothing more important than love, but unfortunately we live in a world where love is lacking.

So many times we search for love in different places, in various people, and in all types of things, hoping to fill a void that only love can satisfy. Usually when we cannot find it in others we turn to "self-love," believing that is what we need to feel complete, but even self-love does not fully fill the emptiness. There has been only one love that has been proven to bring fulfillment. This love affair heals the broken hearted, comforts the lonely, and gives meaning to the lost. I am speaking about the love of God, and I can speak from personal experience, that once I found love in God I never had to look for it in any person, place, or thing again. When I think about God's love for me, many words come to mind. Words such as: **sacrificial.** His love is **selfless.** I can **rely** on it. It is **unchanging.** It is **corrective.** His love is **forgiving;** God's love is **giving,** it is **hopeful,** and it **covers** me. His love is truly **unconditional.**

I was not ready for God's love. For many years I did not know that this type of love was even real. I thought that this type of love was the thing that fairytales were made of. I was only used to the love where something was expected back in return if I gave it. I was familiar with the type of love that was determined by the way someone performed. It was built on conditions. I felt that love had to be earned. I was used to the type of love that was only given out of convenience, but if love meant that I had to be uncomfortable or if I had to make any major adjustments or sacrifices, that is where the love stopped. Becoming ready for God's love totally redefined what I thought love was. Experiencing God's love made me realize that what I was giving to others was not love in any sense of the word.

God's love is **multifaceted**. It showed me what love is. It showed me how I should be loving others, and it proved to me that I am loved. Growing up I did not see the greatest examples of love in my life. The love that I witnessed between my parents looked like a lot of fussing and fighting, yelling and screaming, sadness and anger. The individuals that I believed loved each other were the same ones that were easily angered by each other. The love examples that I saw were filled with pride. They would go days without talking because no one wanted to be the one to apologize or admit that they were wrong. I grew up believing that love went tit for tat, and competed for the Guinness World record of who could keep the longest list of the other person's wrongdoing. By the time I had reached my later adolescent years the love that I watched growing up had failed, and by my early twenties I watched divorce defeat the type love that my parents displayed toward each other. So the task to be re-educated on what love was took deprograming years of learning what love is not.

I tried my hand at *eros love*, that sexual and passionate type of love. That love that throws all caution to the wind and is led by our desires. That love got me nothing but empty pleasure and regret. That love resulted in plenty of heartache for me and for others. The pleasure of eros love exposed me to many dangers and caused me to experiment with many vices, but I eventually discovered that love still did not fill the void. I have also experienced *phila love,* that love that I have for friends in my life. This is a good love but I soon discovered it was only applicable to people that I liked, people that I had things in common with, or people that treated me good. What I noticed was if any of that changed, and they no longer treated me right, this type of love quickly changed and eventually faded away. Eventually I had an opportunity to experience storge love, and I thought that this was the ultimate. I felt that I finally understood what true love was. Storge is that love that we have for our family, especially our children, and when my son was born I felt it. I felt the deepest most intense and protective love for him, just because he existed. He did not have to do anything to earn it and he could not do anything to lose it. In fact we had to do everything for him. All we got in return was another stinky diaper, sleepless nights, and demands to be fed. But my love for him could not be compared to anything that I experienced before. However, even that was not God's love. That Agape love. That love for friends, family, and complete strangers. The love that we receive if we are doing good or doing bad. That love that does not change whether we are at our best or at our worst, if we are sick or if we are healthy. That love that shines through whether we are rich or poor. Agape love, God's love.

This is the love that we must have in order to be ready a relationship. I know that we are only human, and there will always be things that are humanly impossible to achieve. But I figure if we set the bar high enough, and make God's agape love our measuring stick for the way we love others, that will push us to love the person that God has for us to the best of our ability. When the storms of life come we will need that type of love. When we feel disappointed in our mate we will need agape love.

In our relationships there will be disappointments, hurts, and mistakes. In order to have a relationship that will stand the test of time we need agape love, God's love. It will be impossible to develop that level of love for others if we do not get into a relationship with God and get to see how that love works. It was not until I experienced forgiveness for my wrong doing, restoration after I had been unfaithful to Him, and compassion after I hurt Him, before I began to understand exactly what agape love was, and then attempted to emulate it toward others. If we want to be ready for a truly love-filled relationship, we must learn what God's love is.

His Peace

There is a certain level of mental and emotional anxiety that comes with wanting a relationship, but not being able to find what we are looking for. We can grow impatient, frustrated, lonely, hopeless, and discouraged at times. We are not at peace. There is no tranquility within ourselves, and we continue to believe that a relationship with the right man or woman will bring us that internal peace that we are searching for. I used to feel this way. I had similar struggles. I searched for peace in relationships, then I would be disappointed when I realized that the relationship was not bringing me peace. The truth is that I was putting an unrealistic and unreasonable expectation on the relationship and the person I was with. A relationship could not bring me the peace that I needed. I was setting myself up for disappointment and setting up all of my relationships for failure. I would create more stress, I would be more demanding, and I would grow more impatient because I was trying to pull out of people something that only God is able to provide: internal peace.

The best way that I can explain the peace that you find in God is contentment. Contentment is an ease of mind, a peace of mind. It is knowing that regardless of what the situation and circumstance is, was, or will be, all things will work together for good. Whether it be a season of singleness or marriage, a season of plenty or scarcity, a season of loss or a season of gain, God's peace will bring you contentment, trust, and acceptance. When we reach that level of tranquility it shines through our mood and personality. It reflects a calming spirit which brings comfort and encouragement. God's peace will keep you steady through the many storms of life. In a world filled with fears, anger, worries, and anxiety, a peaceful spirit is often needed to bring wisdom and understanding instead of reactiveness and emotions. Being in harmony with God helps to destroy all anger issues. It kills jealousy and the need to control people as well as the need to control the outcome. When I found that peace I learned that many of the problems that I face are not my battle to fight, whether it is being falsely accused, cheated on, lied to, mistreated, let down, or deceived. That peace reminds me that the battle is the Lord's. Becoming ready for God's peace gets us ready to bring that kind of peace, tenderness, and stability into another person's life.

I understand that the things that we go through with dating, love, and relationships can often bring us everything but peace. Relationships can be so difficult at times that we feel that the only way to find God's peace is to stop dating, cut-off any thoughts about a relationship, and completely denounce love. I get it. I have been there and done that. When I decided to stop focusing on relationships I was confusing peace with avoidance, isolation, and fear, which can sometimes feel very peaceful, but it is not the same thing. As I mentioned, the peace that we are looking for is internal. It is a feeling of calm and harmony even when we are in times of trouble. It is not avoiding the storms or hiding from love. The peace of God allows us to be in the storm while preventing the storm from getting into us. The real test of God's peace is when we are able to endure the not-so-good things that come with dating and relationships but still remain balanced mentally, emotionally, and spiritually. Taking a break from dating or relationships for a moment is helpful in gaining God's peace, but to remain in a state of isolation and evasion is not what God wants for us.

God loves relationships, and if we are honest with ourselves, we love them also.

The peace that we find in God is the same peace that we will bring into our relationships. When offenses come, and they will come, we respond in a way that is respectful, logical, constructive, and Godly. When we find that peace in God, we learn to turn to Him when we are faced with the trials and tribulations of relationships and life. We do not put our partner in the unfair position to be the source of our peace. Becoming closer to God brings us closer to that peace that surpasses all understanding. It will become easier to compromise, easier to forgive, easier to make important sacrifices, and easier to communicate about the tough topics in our relationships, because we know that no matter the outcome, things will turn out according to God's plan for our lives. We learn that when we do live according to God's will, it turns out in our favor. That peace and contentment helps us to deal with rejection better, so instead of taking it personal or internalizing the hurt, we conclude that God has given us all the free will to choose who we want and do not want in our lives. He gives us the freedom to have preferences, and we will feel at peace if we are not someone's preference.

We also find hope in the peace that God provides,

a hope that He wants better for us and has better for us, so we learn not to cry over those that have left, but to rejoice over who is to come. I can confess that the more that I have looked to God for my peace, the less stress I feel over dating, relationships, and being single. The more that I experience the peace which comes from developing a relationship with God the more excited I get about being an example of tranquility, contentment, and peace in my future relationship. I can promise that you will find yourself in the same mental and emotional space if you seek your peace from the right place.

His Joy

How many of us are in search of joy? The type of joy that is not based on circumstances. The joy that does not need everything to be perfect in order to exist. The joy that comes from the inside and is felt even when everything is not in our favor. The type of joy that remains even when the feeling of happiness fades away.

Most of us are familiar with the excitement that is felt when things are going our way. We experience delight when something positive happens in our life. But the feeling of being blessed when we are going through challenges, or being in a state of gladness while in the midst of some difficult times is something that we usually do not experience or understand. This is what I call internal joy, the joy of God. His joy that will take us through the worst times, the sick times, and the poorer times that we promise to endure when we make our marriage vows. We enjoy the feeling of happiness that we get from being with our mate, but there will be many times that they will not make us feel happy, and in those times we will have to rely on the source of this internal bliss, which is the joy we find in our relationship with God.

Becoming ready for God's joy has changed my life in such a dramatic way. I have become so much more easygoing because the joy that I find in knowing that God is in control of everything that goes on my life is such a relief. I worry less, my anxieties have lowered, and I am less judgmental of others and myself when things go wrong.

The joy of God has made me more pleasant to be around because it is a joy that cannot be contained. Now I laugh more because I am able to find the comedy in things around me. I am more optimistic because I know what God has promised me. I feel more energized, more focused, and more courageous to go after what I want because I no longer have a happiness that is based on what other people think about me or what other people say about me. I am experiencing a joy that has its foundation set in God.

When we look for joy in people, things, events, and places we are running the risk of making those things an idol. We begin to overvalue the things that make us feel good. We put those things on a pedestal. We view them with so much reverence that it can almost take on a form of worship. This is how we begin to be controlled by others. We wake up one day and find ourselves isolated from love ones, and we feel enslaved to a relationship, because somewhere along the road we thought a man or woman was our only path to happiness and joy. But there is no joy like the one that is found in God. There is no happiness like the one Jesus will bring you. He shows you that He is the Source without using force. It is totally up to us to find the joy of God.

This joy that you find in God will make you better prepared for the relationship that is to come, because you will no longer look for others to be the source of your joy. You will stop putting the weight of such a heavy responsibility on the person that you are with. This joy that you find will come from inside of you. You will no longer blame the person that you are in a relationship with for your moodiness, sadness, and anger. Your expectation of people will be realistic. You will not look for your mate to make you happy and you will not need a mate to be happy. You will not get as hurt and you won't be as surprised when a person does what humans do and that is make mistakes, make poor decisions, or disagree with you, because your inner joy becomes stable. This joy that that is available to us through God can be spread into the lives of others. It will give us the ability to be so much more encouraging because we will feel encouraged. We will become much more optimistic with others because God's joy makes us more optimistic. God's joy takes away the anger, frustration, and insecurities that we used to project on our mate, and He invites us to give it to Him.

There is an old school gospel song that says, "This joy I have, the world didn't give it to me, and the world can't take it away". That lyric sums it up. God's joy will turn you into that individual with an infectious smile. You will become that person whose positive energy can brighten up a room. Instead of looking for your mate to make you happy, you will be the one that brings happiness, excitement, and encouragement in situations that seem bleak. Finding God's joy produces an internal change that makes us a better person and a better mate.

His Patience

We are living a world that seeks after instant gratification. A society where everything is microwaveable. We want our food made and delivered in under twenty minutes, we want our money withdrawn instantly, and we want our prayers answered as soon as we think of them. We lack patience and self-control. We seek to skip the process so we can just get to the end result. There is probably no area of life where we lack patience more than in the area of dating, love, and relationships. We do not like to wait to meet the right person, so we feel it is better to give everyone a chance, as quickly as possible, all at the same time – aka internet dating. We do not like to wait to be intimate so we find ourselves getting sexually connected with someone way before we become spiritually, emotionally, or mentally connected. We do not like to wait for love to grow so we maintain a list of "deal breakers", and as soon as someone goes against our preferences we have a reason to walk away.

I say we because for most of my life I operated in the same mindset. I wanted things now! Ironically, when I decided to enter into a relationship God, I learned the importance of being patient, not only with dating and relationships, but in every aspect of life. *Patience is a virtue* is not just a saying. It is truth. So many times we rush into situations without considering the outcome, in an attempt to fill a void, avoid our feelings, or make a past experience null and void, thinking that jumping into something new is the best way to move past something old. We know all the quotes about patience: "Good things come to those who wait", "Anything worth having is worth waiting for", and "Rome was not built in a day". These are things that I have heard and also said throughout my life, but patience still seemed to elude me when I desired a relationship and when it came to dating. Those sayings were forgotten just as fast as my patience was lost when I saw someone that I wanted. I struggled with delaying gratification. I never tried to subdue my sexual desires. Instead, I fed them more. I was not interested in waiting to meet the right one. I did not have a big enough reason to do so.

Let's be honest: who in their natural mind wants

to delay something that they find pleasurable? Why should we wait to sleep with them? Why wait to buy those shoes, go on that trip, or try that new restaurant, when those things make us happy? It was not until I began to form a deeper relationship with God and His Word, that I began to form a big enough "why" to my waiting, which helped to develop the patience in me. It was when I began to look at my own life and realize that my impatience and need for immediate gratification never got me what I really wanted. Even when I received some level of happiness, the satisfaction that I received was temporary and never as good as I thought it would be. This applied to quick dating, quick intimacy, quick relationships, and when I developed feelings too quickly. I realized that the things that I was in such in a rush to have lost their excitement. I quickly lost interest in them, and the pleasure faded away.

So when I began to replace those other statements such as "good things come to those that wait" with scriptures, it had more power and meaning to me. I found my answer to "why wait" in phrases and verses such as, "wait on the Lord", "be still", "be anxious for nothing", "patience produces character", and "trust in the Lord with all your heart and lean not in your own understanding". I had to make the decision to trust these words, and trust in God's perfect timing. Ultimately, the things that I was waiting for had to change. I no longer was waiting to meet the right woman. I stopped waiting for her to have sex with me. My wait was no longer for the relationship, but I began to wait on God to work in my in my life. It had been proven that I had poor timing. When I moved at my pace, things never turned out right, so I decided to trust more in God's pace. Through developing a stronger relationship with God I have discovered that He will always show up. He will always be there to guide me. He will never leave me alone, and He has always been there when I needed Him. God knows what He is doing and why He is doing it, and trusting in Him helps me to be more patient.

How does this patience look in real life? How will finding God's patience help us to be better prepared for a relationship? For one, it helps us with our own decision making, and it improves our screening process when it comes to meeting someone. It slows us down, and forces us to use our discernment. We see the red flags clearer. We take out the time to study a person's character and we no longer solely go off of the physical things that we see with our eyes, the feelings in our body, and the thoughts in our mind. Now that we are waiting on God's timing we will not have to act out of emotion, no matter what level of relationship we are in. If we are dating and we do not get a call back or an immediate text, we will not allow our minds and feelings to create a story that is based on our own insecurities. We will not self-sabotage by jumping to the conclusion that they no longer like us, they have someone else on the side, or they are trying to have us on the side and have a spouse at home, because with patience we understand that everything is working according to God's perfect timing and not ours. God's patience helps us to deal with facts. It makes sure that our feelings are based on reality and not our own fantasies, because we take out the necessary time to think and process instead of reacting. Learning God's patience kills the urge to make decisions out of desperation, loneliness, boredom, and pressure from others. We put our trust in God's pace and no one else's. It helps to determine if it is the right time to pursue an individual or if we should be pursuing a certain individual at all. We no longer are in a rush to find love. We no longer try to force someone to like us. We truly become content with developing friendships that may or may not lead to more. Patience opens the door to so many opportunities. God's patience with us is the same patience that we must imitate through our process of finding, developing, and maintaining a good relationship.

God's patience is a teaching tool. We are far from perfect, we make mistakes, we intentionally sin, and we can be hurtful and blatantly defiant. God is still patient with us. God's grace and mercy toward us is an example of His patience. He gives us second, third, fourth, fifth, and millions of chances. He is patient with us, and we will need to have that level of patience if we want to be ready for a real relationship. Can we say that we are ready for a relationship if we are the type that seems easily agitated by others, is always impatient and never gives others the time and opportunity to grow, learn, change, or correct a mistake? Bringing those types of qualities into a relationship can destroy it before it even gets started. There is no one created to perfectly fit our every need, want, and desire. There will be disagreements, there will be misunderstandings, and disappointments, and it will take the patience that only comes from God to deal with some of the things that we will face. But if we want to become ready for a relationship we must be ready to face the trials and tests that come with all relationships with patience and trust that God will work things out according to His perfect timing.

His Kindness and Goodness

As I researched for this book and particularly this section, I had some difficulty finding the distinction between *what is kindness* and *what is goodness*. In my mind they were synonymous. All of my life I felt that the two words were interchangeable. If someone appeared to be good I will call them kind, and if someone appeared to be kind I would call them a good person. However as I studied the two words I began to realize that they are quite different. I discovered that goodness is not only a description of the things that we do, but goodness is really about the reasons behind why we do the things that we do, and kindness is not only what we do, but how we do it.

Goodness is a sum of the morals, values, and virtue that influences and molds us. The reason why we do things such as helping an old lady across the street, giving to charity, helping our friends pack and move to their new home, or visiting a sick church member. Goodness is a quality that it sewn into the fabric of our character. Doing things for the betterment of others, not for personal gain or profit. We come across good-hearted people that are very giving of their time, often have a word of positivity and encouragement, and their intentions always seem to be pure and righteous. For example, goodness could be a couple visiting an elderly family member. They are not visiting out of obligation. Their visit isn't done to later brag that they visited. They are not doing it out of guilt because they were forced to. They are visiting the elderly family because they know how lonely it can be and they genuinely want to brighten the family members' day with some company. That is goodness.

Kindness. I found kindness described as the way we do the things that we do, or the spirit and attitude that we have as we complete a task, or provide a service, or help someone. Kindness does not only encompass what we are doing but it takes a closer look at the nature in which we are doing things. Is it done with affection, compassion, grace, and friendliness? We have all come across people that were doing things that are beneficial to others, such as providing a service: a social worker, a mechanic, or doctor for example, but the attitude that they had while doing it was nasty, hard, and unfriendly. Kindness is the opposite of that. Whether it was a waiter at a restaurant or the church usher escorting you to your seat, it is usually the attitude that they project which makes a huge difference. The level of kindness in which someone does things determines how big of tip we might leave, how loved and cared for we might feel, and how encouraged we might be to return the favor. In a world of self-centeredness, impatience, and defensiveness, kindness is an endangered species and it needs to be protected and bred more than ever. There is a difference between kindness and goodness, but this section is not to point out the differences, but to discuss how finding the kindness and goodness of God makes us better prepared to be kind and good toward the person that He is preparing for us.

Now that we have the definition of kindness and goodness, we can understand why these qualities are needed in us if we want to be ready for a relationship, but I will also explain how knowing the definition of goodness and kindness never fully manifested in my life until I began to understand the kindness and goodness of God.

Most of us who grew up in an African-American church recognize the tradition of call and response.

When someone says, "God is good!", we respond, "All the time!" Even though it has become sort of a cliché, it has managed to become one because of the undeniable truth that God is good. How often do we really take the time to meditate on how good and kind God has been to us? As I began to develop a stronger relationship with God, I became more aware of His goodness and kindness. It was not until I became closer to the Lord that I realized how the blessings I received throughout my life have been evidence of His kindness and goodness toward me and not just coincidence, good luck, or results of my hard work. I can think of times when my actions should have and could have landed me in jail, the hospital, or even led to my death, but because of His grace and kindness, mercy and goodness I am still here. His protection and provision are evidence that He is always kind and good, and understanding more about God's goodness and kindness has helped me to treat others with the same treatment that I receive.

How has this experience of God's goodness and kindness helped me, and how can it help us to be better prepared for the relationship that we want? The benefits of being a good and kind person might seem like common sense, but like someone once said, common sense is not always common practice.

In today's society we are simply not good and kind toward each other. We hold on to grudges, we are judgmental, we can be disrespectful, we minimize each other's feelings, and we can be so unforgiving. But when we enter into a relationship with God, and allow His nature to become our own, He begins to create in us a pure heart and renewed mind that spreads to the people in our lives. The goodness that we experience can be seen in the way that God forgives us, comforts us, guides and keeps us, over and over again. This is an example of goodness that we should try to use with our mate. The kindness of God's mercy becomes a part of us. So when we think of how we continue to be blessed, protected, and provided for in spite of our bad decisions or intentional rebellion against God, there is no way we cannot try to have that same grace in our own relationships. When we have experienced the goodness and kindness of God, and the way He keeps doing for us even when we have not worked for it, asked for it, or deserve it, it would be hypocritical for us to enter into a relationship and not to at least try to display that same goodness and kindness toward our mate.

Once I have seen how undeserving I can be of grace, but continue to get it, I feel like it is my obligation to treat the person that God has for me in that same way. That is why these virtues are so important to develop if we want to truly be ready for the relationship we desire. We cannot treat others with meanness, disrespect, and hostility and expect to maintain a healthy relationship. We cannot do things with animosity, selfishness, or only because we expect that it will be done in return and think that someone would want to commit to that type of treatment and atmosphere for the rest of their lives. We must develop genuine goodness and have a pure kindness to be ready. The kindness and goodness that I found in Jesus has set the example for me. Even when we did not want it, He was kind enough come down to save us. Even when we did not deserve it, He was good enough to sacrifice himself for us. Our goodness and kindness may never require us to make that level of sacrifice, but if we can learn to receive what He did for us, we will learn how to do for others in a similar way.

His Faithfulness

A lack of faithfulness might be the leading cause of relationship problems right now. There is very little loyalty and commitment between people. There are those individuals that stand by your side when things are going good, when the sun is shining and the grass is green; but when the times get hard and the friendship gets tested, they are nowhere to be found. In dating and relationships, it is extremely hard to find someone that is willing to stay faithful and committed, someone that will not run and call it quits as soon as they feel uncomfortable, as soon as a problem occurs, or as soon as they no longer feel "happy". A lack of faithfulness is the reason why divorce rates are at an all-time high. A shortage of faithfulness is the reason why the marriage rate has gotten so low. The absence of faithfulness, commitment, and loyalty is the cause for so much pain and heartache in people today. Being ready for a real relationship means that we are ready to be faithful. Not only faithful in terms of fidelity, but also faithful when things are not going the way we expected, faithful when we run into trials and tribulations, and faithful when things go against our preference. The type of faithfulness that God shows us.

Becoming ready for God's faithfulness probably has had the biggest impact on my growth of becoming ready for a relationship. I was what some would call a serial dater. I would meet someone, and date them for some time, but would always find something that I did not like or did not understand about them so that I could end it. I would find a reason to be offended, or a justification to my disappointment, and then cut them off. I would not stick in there and work through the issue. I had no difficulty with finding closure, and then finding someone new. I was not faithful to the process of dating. Totally unfaithful to the development of a relationship. Never faithful to the course that I had to take in order for a deep level of commitment to grow. I had deal breakers, standards, must haves, must nots, top five lists, updateable lists, preferences, wants, needs, you name it. All that did was intellectualize the fact that I had a lack of faithfulness and low tolerance when someone did not perfectly fit into my plan or fulfill my expectations. My family called me picky, and friends called me crazy. It was not until I began to embrace the way God has been faithful to me that I began to understand how weak I was in the area of faithfulness toward others. Through all my shortcomings, all of my disobedience to His plan, all of my rebellion against His will, all of my imperfections, God remains faithful to me.

What if God had a list of deal breakers, must haves, must nots, or a top five list that He used to measure how faithful He would be when loving us? What if He cut us off the minute we did not live up to His expectations or fit in the plans that He has for us? Where would we be? God's faithfulness is consistent, it is stable, it is reassuring, and it is reliable. Whether it is during the times when we are serving Him or the times when we are being totally sinful, He remains dependable. Yes, He allows us to suffer the consequences, and there are moments when He allows us to go through difficulty in order to build our faith and trust, and there are even events when He wants to prove how good and worthy He is, so He permits trials and tribulations to bombard our lives. If you do not believe me, ask Job. But He never leave us, He never forsakes us, He stays by our side, He remains in front of us, and He always has our back. That is faithfulness. Through

His example of faithfulness, we learn to be faithful to others. We learn to be true in friendships, devoted to family, and committed in relationships with the ones we love. That faithfulness that we experience as we grow deeper with God actually sheds light on how imperfect we are and then it sheds light on how His faithfulness does not shake. His steadfastness makes us more aware of our shortcomings which then makes us more aware of how God's devotion to us never weakens. Becoming ready for God's faithfulness made me more ready for a relationship. His faithfulness allowed me to gain real life experience of what true commitment is, what real devotion looks like, and what unbreakable support feels like.

The root word of faithfulness is faith. Now when we speak of God's faith, it puts a different spin on what I have been speaking about in this section, but it is just as needed for those of us that want to become relationship ready. Strengthening my relationship with God also gave me a better understanding of God's faith. God's faith is believing that His promises will happen even when we do not know how. It is the understanding that all good things will come to pass, and knowing that all things will work together for the good even when we do not see it with the naked eye. Learning God's faith brings a natural sense of optimism, belief, and favor to any relationship. Faith gives us confidence that things will work out during times of trouble. God's faith helps us to search for solutions and not dwell on the problem when we experience conflict. God's faith stops us from making a mountain out of a molehill because we believe that things will work out for the better. Being ready for a relationship requires us to bring that level of faith; building a relationship with God helps us to develop that level of faith. We cannot enter into relationships with disbelief, doubt, limits, and pessimism. That only leads to negativity and self-sabotage. That makes us look out for the bad and anticipate that things will go wrong, which will poison any relationship. His faithfulness and His faith is needed to be ready for a relationship.

To sum up this section, I first want to be sure that you do not misunderstand what I previously wrote. I am not saying that we should not have any standards or deal breakers, or that we should accept or endure wrong treatment. But I am saying we should let those must have's, deal breakers, and top five lists be based on Godly criteria and spiritual truths, and not our own superficial desires. If we want to be ready for a relationship, we must be ready to be faithful. We cannot walk around being faithless, disloyal, untrustworthy, and changeable and believe that we are ready to be in a healthy relationship. Faithfulness is needed more than anything if we are looking to develop love, because love is many things. Love is patient, it is kind, it is giving, it is forgiving, it does not fail; but nowhere does it says that love is easy. It does not say that love will not have its problems and tough times, and that is when our faithfulness comes into play. That is when we will need the type of faithfulness that only God can give us.

His Gentleness

When we hear the word gentle, what do we often think of? Many of us might think: weak, soft, a pushover, or someone that can be easily taken advantage of. Gentle is not something that many of us aspire to be. We admire those that are aggressive, assertive, speak their minds, and have the ability to verbally or even physically break another person down. Gentleness has seemed to lose its place in today's society. Even as believers, we see gentleness as a passive quality, even when the One that we claim to follow and believe in was a gentle soul. Jesus handled people with a sweet gentle spirit, even those that constantly opposed him.

In relationships, we often hear that the "take charge" type of man, the type that knows how to put a woman in her place when needed is the most desirable type. We have forgotten how much gentleness is needed in our lives. We have allowed gentleness to lose its importance in our relationships, parenting, friendships, and leadership. We fail to realize that in order to be understanding of others it takes gentleness. In order to be a good communicator it takes gentleness. We cannot be forgiving without first learning to be gentle. It is impossible to be empathic to the issues of others if we do not have a gentle heart. To be compassionate, it takes gentleness. We try to influence others through the use of force, but it takes gentleness to really get people on our side. We would like to connect with people by showing strength, but it takes gentleness to experience true intimacy.

Gentleness did not come easy for me. I grew up in a community where being humble, calm, and sensitive could lead to a person becoming a victim, so we learned to handle everything with aggression, violence, and vigor. The way I walked, talked, even looked had to be packed with aggressive power. Add that need for hardness based on safety to the social conditioning that I experienced promoting machismo. I was taught that there is very little place for sensitivity in manhood. So you can only imagine how gentleness is a characteristic that I did not put much time into developing. In sports I was taught to be aggressive in order to win. With friendships, I learned that being the strongest gave me the greatest chance of being the leader. When dealing with women I was taught that the opposite of fear was aggression so I would approach a young lady with force, to show that I was not scared and that I was in control.

There once was a time that this would only describe men, but in today's world many women have taken on these same characteristics of aggressiveness, insensitivity, and force. Gone are the days when a young lady would wait for a guy to approach her. In today's society, being gentle means that you could lose out, so women are going after the man that they want in higher numbers.

It took some time, maturity, and an understanding of God's will to realize that there is more strength in gentleness than in my aggression and toughness. It took me building a relationship with God to see that real power and wisdom comes in the ability to handle situations and people with soft hand and tender tongue. It took coming into the knowledge of God's gentleness to understand that I needed a compassionate heart and considerate mind in other to be ready for the one that He wanted to bring into my life.

The way we respond to each other when problems, disagreements, and disconnections occur can be the thing that either makes or breaks a relationship, or at least makes a relationship very hard or very delightful to be in. It is the trials and tribulations that we face during dating and relationships which test the strength of our bond. I always say, we do not know what our relationship is really made of until we face our first issue. Whether it is something as serious as when someone is sick, loses a job, or the death of a love one; or something that seems as trivial as not returning a call, being late for a date, wanting to go to two different restaurants, or not changing one's Facebook status. Without the ability to deal with each other with gentleness and sensitivity, something that may seem as trivial as returning a text can turn into a full blown argument or even a break up.

It is not in our nature to be gentle or sensitive when things are not going our way, or when people are not going our way. Only God teaches us to do something as unnatural as to love your enemies, bless those that curse you, do not repay evil for evil, be slow to anger, and to consider it joy when we face trials. That takes gentleness, a gentleness that only comes through forming a relationship with God. The type of gentleness that we need in order to be ready for a relationship. It takes a gentle spirit to respect your man when he has disappointed you. It takes a soft heart to continue to love your lady when you feel disrespected. We must be sensitive in our speech even when our mate says or does something that infuriates us, because dealing with these issues with aggression, force, and dominance only fuels the fire that will eventually burn the relationship to the ground. The gentleness of God can only be learned when we are ready for God, and being ready for God help us to become ready for a relationship.

There are so many examples of how Jesus dealt with issues with gentleness. Do you remember the time when the woman was caught in adultery and the people brought her to Jesus for judgment? By law she could have and should have been stoned to death, but Jesus said to those that brought her, "he that is without sin, throw the first stone", and He told her to leave and sin no more – that's gentleness. Or how about the demon possessed man that lived in the tombs, that everyone tried to bind, subdue, and chain. How did Jesus deal with him? Jesus was compassionate enough to see that the man was living in torment, and gentle enough to empathize with his hurt. He set the man free from his pain and torture. The man that once struck fear in the hearts of the people was found peacefully sitting at the feet of Jesus, begging to follow Him, and the man's life was changed. That is gentleness.

Gentleness builds intimacy. It helps people to let

down their guard and become more vulnerable. What type of relationship would we be ready for if we remain easily agitated, cruel, harsh, and irritable? Who would want to be in a relationship with someone that has that type of behavior or constant mood? A gentle spirit is inviting. It allows others to feel comfortable, less judged, and it encourages your partner to be themselves with you. If you learn to apply the gentleness of God in your life, you will see your relationships elevate to a new level.

Self-Control or His Control

Self-control has seemed to become such a negative concept in today's world. Popular terms like, "YOLO: You only live once" and "life is short", promote the idea that we should do whatever makes us happy, and our constant search for pleasure and gratification has really penetrated our view of what life should be. Self-control does not seem fun. It is not exciting. It almost makes us feel trapped. People like to let loose, live freely, and let down their hair and inhibitions.

Every day we are faced with a choice. That choice is, are we going to be self-controlled or outer-controlled? Will we practice restraint or allow our impulses and natural desires to lead the way? We have to decide if our decisions will be based off of what we need, what is right, what we believe in, and what we know to be true, or if we will allow our decisions to be based on what we want, what we prefer, and what we think we can get away with. It is truly an internal battle between right or wrong, the light or darkness. Yes, we all have a Luke Skywalker and a Darth Vader living inside of us.

As I mature and grow to understood the difference between self-control and outer-control, I am realizing that for me, there is not really a huge difference between the two. When given the opportunity I discovered that I would prefer to seek out pleasure, just like most would. I would allow the excitement of having fun to control me just like everyone else would. I had a tendency to go with my impulses and desires just like everyone around me. I realized when I controlled myself, I often would journey to the dark side or at least toe the line so closely that I was able to hop back and forth when it was convenient. After some time, I eventually learned that even self-control is only good depending on who or what we allow to control us.

Self-control is guided by the principles, values, and desires that we feel are important. If my desires and values are not pure and righteous what good is self-control? It no longer became a decision of whether I practice self-control or outer-control. It turned into me practicing self-control or God's-control.

In order to be ready for the relationship that God has for us, self-control will not do; at least not in the way that we understand it. The reason is, if we rely on ourselves there is a good chance that we will react in anger, be impatient, be unfaithful, or allow our emotions to get the best of us. We have to look toward a Being that is bigger and better than us to help keep ourselves under control. In essence, self-control is not allowing ourselves to lead the way or relying on ourselves to take control and make the decisions, but self-control is really keeping yourself under control. That is, minimizing our impulses, suppressing our natural desires, and starving the decisions that we want to make. We have probably heard some pray, "help me to decrease so that God can increase". Those are the powerful words of John the Baptist found in the New Testament. That is the true meaning of self-control. The decrease of oneself so that God can take control.

God's-control is more than saying "No" to our impulses and denying ourselves of what we desire; that is only half of the job. God's-control is not complete until we begin to say "Yes" to His will and plan for our lives. In a relationship it is not enough for a man to not lie to his mate. It is not enough that he does not cheat on his fiancé, and it great that he does not abuse his wife, but his job is not done just because he says no to those things. His responsibility is not met until he says yes to God's will. By saying yes to God's will, that means that he will love his wife as Christ loves the church. He has to take the next step and treat her as the gentler vessel, which means treating her with understanding, sensitivity, and tenderness. That is being God-controlled. It is not enough for a woman to control her impulses to say something out of line to her husband. Her job is not complete because she stopped emasculating her fiancé. Just like the man, she has to follow God's will by honoring and respecting him. She has to do and say things that will lift him up, support, and encourage him. The Bible says that power of life and death lies in the tongue, so yes, she might have stopped killing him by no longer tearing him down with her mouth, but is she being God-controlled and giving him life by choosing to lift him up and affirming him with that same tongue? These are things that self-control does not push us to do, but God-control does. These are the things that can change a stale unfulfilling relationship, into a joyful, healthy, and enriching one. In order for me to let go of self-control and begin to embrace God's-control, I had to begin to trust God more. I had to trust that what He says is true, and that His promises are real. I had to believe that once I received God's love that

I would no longer need to search for love in all of those empty damaging people, places, and activities that I used to search for it. I had to trust that finding my joy in God was better than the happiness that I tried to create for myself. I truly had to believe that basking in the peace that comes with a relationship with God is better than any temporary relief that I experienced with others. Trusting in the faithfulness, kindness, and gentleness of God brought me the security and assurance that I needed to be ready for the relationship that He has for me.

As I said in the beginning of this chapter, if I could put it all in one statement, I would say, "Find it in God and you will never have to look for it in man", meaning mankind. Finding it in God does not take away our desire to be in a relationship. It does not mean that I will no longer want companionship and commitment. But it does mean that I will no longer be needy for it. I will no longer be desperate or thirsty for it. I will be coming to the relationship complete, whole, and full. I will not depend on my mate to bring me joy; instead I will spread the joy that I already have. I will not come into any relationship looking for my mate to create peace in my life because I will come with the peace of God that is infectious in a relationship. I will no longer hunger after the feeling and need to be loved, because I will come into the relationship with the confidence, worthiness, and experience of knowing that I have the greatest love of all. Being ready for a relationship with God made me ready for a relationship with the person that God will bring into my life, and it will do the same for you.

3. Know Thyself

In Erikson's stages of psychosocial development, he labels our adolescent years as the identity versus role confusion stage. In this phase of life, the task is to successfully explore and grow into who we will be as a person. We discover different interests, our worldview starts to take shape, and we begin to understand our likes and dislikes. During this time, we start to identify the issues that are important to us, and we gravitate toward the values that seem to be true and beneficial to our way of living. It is said that this stage is the foundation of who we will eventually be for the rest of our lives. We begin to form thoughts and beliefs that are independent from what our parents taught us when we were younger. According to this theory, those that fail to successfully transition through this stage are considered to be in an "arrested development," where their maturation becomes stagnant, and their growth is stuck at that level. Arrested development increases the probability that they will struggle with their identity as an adult.

When we do not know who we are, it is very difficult to know what to accept in or reject out of our lives, especially when it comes to relationships. We end up experimenting with our hearts, we take major chances with our bodies, or we roll the dice with our mind and emotions in hopes that we will get lucky. We find ourselves in an identity crisis. Not knowing who we are, hiding who we are, or being in denial of who we are. If we cannot be real with ourselves because we do not know ourselves, how will we ever be real in a relationship? When I say real I don't mean "keeping it real", but I am referring to real honesty, real vulnerability, real comfort, real love. This crisis brings us to our second key of relationship readiness: the need to know thyself.

At times we do not know where we come from, we do not know where we are going, and we do not know why we are here. Some identity loss can be attributed directly to a systematic plan to rob a person, a culture, or a group of people of true their identity. At other times it could be the circumstances that we are born in which force us into a certain identity that is not aligned with our heart, and then there are times when we wasted years establishing our identity in foolish, temporary, and superficial things which led to a life of confusion and misfortune. No matter which road brings us to this point in life, now is the time to chart a different course.

In order to be truly ready for a healthy relationship we must travel the road of self-discovery, self-acceptance, self-actualization, self-esteem, self-worth, self-congruency, self-love, and self-discipline. In order to be ready for a relationship we must know who we are so that we can better determine what we want and do not want so we can also bring all of our gifts, talents, and individuality to benefit a relationship.

Ready for Self-Discovery

It is impossible to know who we are if we have never taken out the time to truly search ourselves. Self-discovery is not something that we can just stumble upon. It takes focus, intention, and time. So many of us have allowed outside forces to dictate who we are, who we should be, and who we will be, and now we live in complete and utter confusion because we have allowed different voices to penetrate our soul. Maybe it was our parents pushing us into a career a choice that we really did not want, or maybe we allowed societal or religious traditions to control our personality and character. Perhaps we were molded by the malicious hands and words of an abuser, an inappropriate touch of someone we trusted, or the neglectful absence of someone who was supposed to take care of us. Whatever happened, it resulted in us not feeling confident and comfortable in who we are.

We walk around every day not knowing our true selves and not knowing what we are supposed to be doing with our lives. When we do not take out the time to discover meaning and purpose for our own lives, we end up seeking out relationships hoping that the relationship will give our lives meaning. Which consequently keeps us in a rotation of senseless and meaningless connections with people who are not in harmony with our destiny or identity.

We must realize that no one else can make us into who we are supposed to be. We will continue to feel unfulfilled if we do not take out the time to discover what satisfies and fills us. We will always struggle with a feeling of inadequacy if we never find out what makes us so unique and significant. Some of us are afraid to go on the path of self-discovery because we are scared of what we might find. We try to bury certain experiences in the past, and we numb ourselves to painful memories, not realizing that this is only working against us. If we dig through that pain we've been avoiding, if we begin to feel the emotions that we have numbed, and if we uncover those memories we will find the answers and as a result we will find ourselves.

The road to self-discovery can be a difficult journey because it is full of twists and turns, peaks and valleys, but this is a journey that we must take if we ever want to truly know ourselves. We must go on this discovery expedition in order to be ready for the type of relationship that we pray for. Once we discover who we really are, we will have the ability to become a blessing to a relationship rather than always looking to be blessed.

Self-discovery is uncomfortable. It will shed light on things from our past that we have been trying to hide in shadows. Self-discovery can be lonely. There will be times when we have to isolate our minds, bodies, and souls so the only voice that is influencing us is God's. Self-discovery is exciting because it opens up a whole new world to us: it reveals our gifts, talents, passions, and it helps us to find our purpose. It will be strange and full of surprises because each new door that opens leads to another door as we find out how complex and hurt, gifted and damaged, blessed and troubled we really are. Yes, we will have to face the good as well as the bad aspects of our lives as we self-discover.

You might be wondering what is needed to begin this road toward self-discovery? The beauty of it all is that everybody's journey is different. Some people have been able to do it through prayer and meditation. They came to the understanding that the key to self-discovery lies within, and all they needed to do was examine themselves. Others traveled to a distant land or maybe they just sat at the pond in the park, but they took out the time to think, talk to God, listen to what He was saying, and decided to take action. Some people have found themselves with the help and support of others. Perhaps they sought out a good therapist, or they received spiritual counseling from clergy. Others have taken the journey with a trusted friend or family member who helped them to identify their identity. There is no cookie cutter way to self-discovery. We have to find the road that best fits us. The one thing that is common in every journey is that it starts with a decision. We must choose the journey of self-discovery. We have to get to the point where we are tired of walking around in a fog, looking for other people to give our life meaning or blaming others for our life not having any meaning. We have to get to the point where we no longer will allow fear of criticism, fear of standing out, fear of failure, or even fear of success to stop us from discovering our place in this world. We must eliminate the habits, the people, and the negative thinking that sabotage our growth. We compare ourselves to others. We become discontent with our lives. We allow envy and jealousy to control the way we feel about ourselves. All of these things can contribute to our identity loss and confusion.

Becoming ready to discover who we are is so vital to being ready for a relationship. We often hear people say that they lost themselves in a relationship, but chances are that they never knew who they truly were going into the relationship and that is why they were consumed by another person's life, personality, and goals. A relationship should help us become a greater version of ourselves, not become a different version of your mate. However, when we do not have an identity and life of our own, it becomes easier to take on someone else's. Discover who you are first, so when it's time to be in that relationship we dreamed about it will truly be two individuals coming together as one. We will be able to enhance the life of our mate because we have discovered our purpose, we discovered our talents, we discovered gifts, we discovered us.

Ready for
Self-Acceptance

So many times we try to ignore our reality just so that we can preserve the fantasy we've created. We refuse to accept our lot in life. We try to reject who we are and we attempt to deny what we have done. We would rather blame and accuse others for our circumstances and condition. A huge part of knowing ourselves is getting to the stage of self-acceptance, where we are able to admit where we fall short, embrace the areas that we are weak in, and be responsible for the choices that we have made.

When I speak about self-acceptance I choose to come from the perspective of weakness and error because we rarely have a problem accepting our strengths and good decisions. Self-acceptance is a key step in knowing yourself. Without self-acceptance we will never improve in the areas that we are deficient, we will never heal the parts that are broken, and we will even struggle to celebrate the things that are great about us. We see all the time, some of the most attractive people getting cosmetic surgery. Individuals pretending to be someone they aren't because they are ashamed of their flaws.

In order to be ready for a relationship we must be ready for self-acceptance. We must embrace all sides of us, the good as well as the bad. The evolved us as well as the immature us. The sanctified side as well as the sinful side. The truth is that we all are made up of different layers, and we must be ready to accept ourselves the way that we are before we try to make changes. Our physical imperfections, our background, different life experiences, and our failures are a part of what makes us the person that we are today. Change and improvement is always possible, but the first step to any improvement is self-acceptance.

No matter how perfect and put together we think we are or show ourselves to be, there is always a side that we try to hide from the world, and that is usually the side that we refuse to accept. We might be successful in hiding it from strangers or masking it from co-workers and our neighbors, but we cannot deceive ourselves, and we definitely cannot hide it from our Creator. If we decide to enter into a relationship, it will also be impossible to hide it from our mate forever. Self-acceptance is important for individual growth. Without it we will remain in a state of powerlessness, where we feel that everything and everyone around us has control over who we are. Self-acceptance is important to spiritual growth, because if we never accept who we are and the errors we have made, we will never become open to the person that God made us to be. Self-acceptance is so important when it comes to relationships because it is closely tied to our ability to be vulnerable. We will never show the person who we're with who we truly are if we are not willing to accept our truth. How will we ever receive that unconditional love that we hope for if we are never open enough to show our insecurities, fears, and blemishes?

In dating we often have issues with someone presenting their "representative". This is when someone tends to put his or her best foot forward during the initial stage of dating. They are attentive, kind, available, agreeable; they show all of their good qualities or at least the qualities that we want to see. As time goes on, we begin to see sides of them that are not as pleasant and endearing. That is when we say, the first one was the "representative". Now there are some people that are strictly out to deceive and they must be dealt with accordingly. But I would like to think that most people seeking a relationship are fundamentally good and are not out to intentionally mislead others, but they have not been through the process of self-acceptance, and they have not accepted their own flaws, so they try to hide them. They are not real about their shortcomings so they embellish them. Their actions are more about their discomfort with self and less about the person they are dating being tricked.

Self-acceptance addresses this in two ways. When I have accepted who I am as a person, both my strengths and flaws, I am less worried about others accepting me. My fear of rejection decreases dramatically, and I feel more free to be myself. I no longer try to appear perfect because I have grown comfortable with my imperfections. So the person you meet during week one of dating will be the same basic person you know during week twelve of dating. On the other side of the coin, I grow in grace when I have accepted myself. Meaning, when I do see a different side of someone I am not as fast to label them as fake or deceitful because I understand that other people are flawed just like I am, and I do not expect them to fit into this false idea of perfection that I have created in my mind. So when I see a side that I never saw before I view it as a different side and not as offended or emotionally reactive, because I understand that I also have layers.

That grace allows us to truly get to know an individual. That grace helps us to develop our forgiveness. That grace helps us to not turn every little thing that goes against our preferences into a deal breaker. That grace frees people to be themselves. We need that grace if we ever want to be in a solid long lasting relationship. Do not get me wrong: with grace must come discernment so that we are able to determine when it is just another side of a generally good person or if they are actually trying to hurt us or intentionally deceive us.

Self-acceptance is the key to self-improvement. In order to be ready for a relationship, we must be ready to accept our weaknesses so that we can work on them. It is not a sign of failure or impairment to admit where we are deficient, but not accepting that side of us actually leaves us more powerless because it puts the responsibility of fixing what needs to be fixed on someone else. Self-acceptance is empowering. It gives us permission to take control of our own lives. It prepares us to face whatever the future holds, whether it is our careers, health, or a relationship. When we begin to accept ourselves our perspective begins to change. What we thought was a flaw is the thing that makes us unique. What seemed like fear is what powers our discernment and intuition. Our failures become our practice toward perfection. Our background becomes the springboard that launched us toward our destiny. When we are ready to accept who we are the world has no choice but to follow suit.

Ready for Self-Actualization

If self-discovery is finding the ingredients we need to make the cake, and self-acceptance is the instructions to mix, pour, and stir, then self-actualization is putting the cake in the oven to bake. Self-actualization is making the decision to walk in our destiny. It comes after we discover, then accept, and now we are ready to be who we were created to be. We are ready to go through the fire and rain to fulfill our purpose. It is when we start to do what needs to be done so the dreams and goals that we have for ourselves are accomplished. It is more than saying, "I am special" or thinking "I am worthy". Self-actualization is the behavioral, spiritual, and mental changes we make to be special and worthy. Self-actualization does not only mold us into who we really are, but it shows the world what we are made of.

When it comes to relationships we truly do not know what type of mate we need or what type of mate we will be until we begin live out our purpose, because our purpose is what defines our lives. Allow me to compare our actualization to being in a science class, where we discover that there is a difference between learning the theory of spontaneous combustion and going into the lab and mixing the chemicals that create spontaneous combustion. Reading this book, listening to motivational talks, and creating self-affirming statements is the classroom work. Self-actualization is going into the lab of life and setting it on fire. Self-actualization is doing the work.

I know that many of us choose to operate on the "name it and claim it" theory. While there is power in auto suggestion and self-talk, the process of self-actualization takes more. It takes self-talk and a self-walk to self-actualize. Saying that I am a doctor does not make me a doctor. Believing that I am a Christian does not make me a Christian, just like saying, "I am a queen or king" does not make us royalty. There needs to be proof. We need to bear fruit. We need to act out who and what we say we are in order for actualization to take place.

This is the moment when we truly explore what we like and don't like. We gain real life experience with what works for us and what does not. Once this process is complete, when someone comes to us with something that goes against what we need or want we are able to immediately say, "That's not for me". Or when someone comes requiring something from us that we cannot provide we are able to say, "Sorry I am not able to give that to you". These are some of the great benefits of self-actualization. We are able to walk in our truth. We do not try to fill a void in another person's life that we do not have the ability or responsibility to fill, and we do not try to fill the void in our lives with something that does not fit. If you know that you are not able to be a therapist and a lover to someone that's emotionally broken, when you are self-actualized, you do not try to be. When we know that we do not have the capacity to be the financer for someone that is jobless, we never attempt to be their financial support. Knowing ourselves is knowing that we cannot be the mother or father to someone that is looking to be taken care of. It also teaches us that we cannot find a replacement mother or father to fill in where ours was missing. When we try to be someone or something that we were never created to be, that does not create love; it creates co-dependency and turns you into an enabler.

How many times have we tried to be something

for someone that we were never meant to be? What would you say was the reason? What was the result? If we knew who we were, would we have tried to be someone or something that we were not? Something to think about.

As we self-actualize and walk in our callings, we grow more and more confident in who we are as individuals. As a result, we live with purpose. We live without the fear or concern of what others think of us, and it is that confidence which activates the law of attraction. It draws people to us who are like minded and who like us for who we are. It is assurance of who we are which makes us ready for who is for us. It is the perfect complement to someone that needs what you bring to the table. A character and quality that our future mate will admire and appreciate. Are you ready? Are ready to become who you already know you are? In order to be ready for a relationship we must be ready to be ourselves. We must be ready to unmask and unhide. We must walk in our purpose if we want the right person to walk into our lives.

Ready for Self-Improvement

Accepting who we are is one thing. Improving on who we are is an entirely different process that we must choose to go through when we are serious about getting ready for a relationship. Self-improvement is not about being the perfect partner, but self-improvement is about becoming the best possible version of who we are. It is making an effort to be the person that we need to be, being the change that we want to see, and fulfilling the potential that we want to reach. Self-improvement is about raising the bar and lifting our standards so that we can give the world a better rendition of ourselves.

I regularly hear the idea that if someone loves a person that they should accept them just as they are, flaws and all. It is time to stop using the excuse of unconditional love as a rationale behind our refusal to do better. I am sometimes amazed by the conditions, the behaviors, and the attitudes that singles expect others to accept and live with, just to be with them. Then when the individual refuses to be in a relationship with them because of that behavior or attitude, they feel that the individual could not accept them for who they were. Or they spiritualize it and say "it's not my season", or that it was not ordained by God. The truth is, we might enter our season if we change our behavior. God might ordain it if we improve our attitude. But so many of us want to change and improve our circumstances without having to change or improve ourselves.

I believe the refusal to self-improve is a major reason why people settle in relationships. It is not always due to a lack of good prospects or loneliness. Many settle because it is a reflection of what we do with our own lives. We become comfortable, we adjust to our flaws, and we do not look to change or improve so it is only natural that the same attitude is manifested in our relationships. Show me a person that is always looking to improve themselves and I'll show you someone that doesn't settle for any old type of relationship just to say that they have a one.

I was once told that when we are making a decision to enter into a relationship, we must accept that individual for the man or woman that they are

today, because they may never change. I understand
the thought behind that sentiment, but change is
inevitable. Even a person's refusal to change and
evolve will create a change in a relationship. If one
partner is growing, learning, maturing and the other
partner is not willing to change, that will create
change in the relationship. As we come to that point
of self-acceptance and we begin to grow in grace as
we discussed in the previous section, both our grace
and our partner's grace will reach its limitation if
we never try to improve the areas of our lives that
prevent our relationship from growing to a higher
level. Whether that area is poor money
management, poor communication skills, poor
prioritization, lack of affection, a wandering eye, or
being emotionally unavailable, we will eventually
have to try to improve in the areas that we are weak
in. If we do not, they will eventually make our
relationship weaker, and if you are not in a
relationship yet, it will always stop you from being in
the great relationship that you desire to be in.

What does it take to begin self-improving? It takes
self-discipline. All of us have certain habits that we
know we must stop because those habits get in our
way of being the best possible version of ourselves.
We all have habits that we should start practicing in
order to rise to the best possible version of ourselves.

That moment when we become serious about making real changes in our lives, we become honest with ourselves, and we develop the discipline that is needed in order to make the change possible. For example, for years I wanted to write a book. It has always been a dream of mine, but the time kept passing me by and I had not even written the first sentence. It was not until I became serious about eliminating certain habits out of my life and adding other habits into my life that I began to make progress and see my dream come to reality. I do not know what those habits are for you, but for me I had to become more disciplined in so many areas. In order to write this book, I had to become disciplined with my sleep. I had to go to bed at a certain time so I could wake up early enough to work on my dream every morning before I went to work. I had to become more disciplined with my entertainment. In order to self-improve so that I could reach my goal, studying and research became my entertainment, so there are several popular television shows that I have never seen one episode of. There are several football and basketball games that I have missed, and many social gatherings that I did not attend, because I had to discipline myself. By eliminating some of the more pleasurable entertainment and by adding studying, research, reading, and writing I was able to achieve this goal. My whole point is that the same applies to us when it comes to any kind of self-improvement. It is going to take discipline, it will take sacrifice, and it will take dedication. It takes the same type of disciplined sacrifice and practice to be ready for a healthy relationship.

The self-discovery process reveals to us where we need to become more disciplined in order to be the best possible versions of ourselves. With self-improvement we have discovered the habits we must break and we identify the habits we must start.

That "man in the mirror moment" usually begins us on the path of self-improvement because unfortunately, many of us do not get to that moment until we have experienced some pain or disappointment from trying to live the status quo. It usually isn't until we feel discomfort and become sick and tired of being sick and tired and we decide to improve our situations. The man that has left a trail of broken hearts and bruised emotions during his escapades of self-indulgence usually will not seek to improve until he experiences that same pain that he had been inflicting on others. That woman that has been attracted to "bad boys" will not improve her decision making and change her selection process until she gets tired of the heartache, disappointment, and conflict that dating the type that she lusts after leads to. It is when we have that man in the mirror moment – that is when we will begin our journey toward self-improvement.

The key is that we have to want to self-improve. We have to realize that we have the power to change the things we have discovered in our lives that we do not like, or even the things that we like but we realize are getting in the way of achieving a bigger and better purpose. On social media I often see the question asked, "Would you trade social media for a happy relationship?" That is what I mean by exchanging the thing that we like for something that we feel is better, more beneficial, and more fulfilling. So the question is, what tendencies, characteristics, habits, or even addictions do we have to change in order to be ready for the type of relationship that we want to be in? We all have room to improve. We can turn bad into good; if we are good we can become great, and if we are great we can strive for excellence.

Ready for Self-Esteem

Why do we allow negative treatment from others?

Why do we make excuses for people that intentionally take advantage of us?

Why do we continuously expose ourselves to toxic individuals?

Why do we feel that we do not deserve to be happy?

Allow me to summarize it in a single word: Self-esteem. I think it is safe for me to say that most people understand how our self-esteem has a direct effect on how we experience the relationships in our lives, and the way we have experienced relationships has a direct effect on our level of self-esteem. Whether it be the relationships with our parents, friends and family, a teacher, or a mate, they all can have a positive or negative impact on our self-esteem. This impact affects the way we function in all relationships. Self-esteem is a combination of how we feel about ourselves, the way we think about ourselves, and the perspective in which we view ourselves. It controls the manner in which we treat ourselves, and that dictates how we allow others to treat us.

A low self-esteem might be the foundation for every abusive relationship that we find ourselves in, and it is more than likely the source of most of the terrible decisions we make when it comes to selecting the wrong mate. When we have a poor self-esteem we feel undeserving of a relationship so we end up doing any and everything to keep someone in our lives, even when the person is making us feel depressed, inferior, and helping us to self-destruct. We compromise our morals and values. We ignore the red flags and warning signs. We re-traumatize ourselves by entering a cycle of abuse, over and over again. These are all connected to a broken self-esteem.

To be ready for a healthy relationship, we must have a positive self-esteem. We must have a strong self-image. We must practice encouraging self-talk, and we have to have a good concept of self. It all falls under the umbrella of knowing thyself, the true self that the Creator made us to be, and not the less-than self which the negative and wicked have tried to make us believe that we are.

REBUILDING MY SELF-IMAGE

In a world that holds physical appearance at such a high level of importance there is no surprise that our self-image and self-esteem are so closely connected. Society has created a standard of beauty that the majority has decided to follow, and for those of us that fall outside of that standard, there is a real potential to develop a major complex regarding the way we look and the way we see ourselves as a whole. The world says that a certain weight, a certain height, a certain complexion, eye color, hair length, body shape, set of teeth, nose shape, jaw bone, cheek bone, eyebrow arch, eyelash, muscular frame, facial hair, shoes, pants, shirt, dress, pair of panties, bra, or boxers is what makes one attractive. That list may sound exaggerated, but it really is not. We really do pick ourselves apart on every detail of how we look, and many of us actually live our lives trying to check off everything on that list to make sure we reach the standard. The young and not-so-young have developed a damaged self-esteem because they have not met that standard.

There are so many that feel left out, depressed,

unaccepted, or have pushed themselves to sickness and even death trying to achieve this standard of beauty. If you fall in that category, it is time to realize that in order to receive the love and relationship we desire, we must first love what we see when look at ourselves, inside and out. We cannot change the world's standard because the world will do what it wants to do, but it is time to realize that we do not have to subscribe to that standard. We can create our own. We can embrace what makes us special, and we can live up to our own uniqueness. So if your standard is to be a certain weight that is fine. Or maybe you want to wear a certain kind of lipstick – that is great. The key is, it's your standard of beauty and not anyone else's.

We must reach the point where we are satisfied with what we see when we look at ourselves, because self-doubt and being self-conscious about our self-image is contagious. Others feel and see our insecurity just as much as we feel and see it. Are you ready? Ready to set your standard, ready to meet your own approval, and as the makeup ad says, ready to, "love the skin you're in".

CHANGING MY SELF-TALK

Our self-talk goes hand and hand with our self-esteem. The thoughts that we have toward ourselves, the words that we write about ourselves, and the messages that we repeat to ourselves about ourselves is what ultimately develops our self-esteem. A person can try to tell us what we are and what we are not for our entire lives, but it will have little to no effect on our self-esteem until we begin to tell ourselves that same message. So the question is, what are we telling ourselves about ourselves? All day long we are receiving suggestions about who and what we should be – the voices of our parents, pastors, partners, commercials, social media... Everyone has an opinion. Some messages are as direct and cruel as the one our ex gave which said, "You are worthless and no one else will ever love you!", and other messages are more indirect and subliminal like a television ad which somehow communicates our inadequacies, feeds our jealousy, and creates envy when we see what we do not have. The danger is when we take these messages personally and begin to apply them to our belief system. We repeat these messages to ourselves and internalize the thought of not being good enough, smart enough, pretty enough, rich enough, or whatever the message might be. Our self-talk makes all of the difference.

The things that we tell ourselves can either push

us to great achievements or hold us back from doing something as simple as smiling and saying hello. For example, if we are telling ourselves, "People do not like me", "I'll never fit in", and "No one understands me", we will begin to reflect that in the way we interact with others, and it will become a self-fulling prophesy which stops you from saying hello, and stops you from liking others, and stops you from fitting in.

For those of us that find ourselves repeating those negative self-affirmations, and constantly rehearsing the messages of fear, doubt, deficiency, it is time to combat those thoughts. There is an internal battle going on inside of our minds and it is time to call reinforcements to win the war. We must be ready to change our self-talk, and speak to ourselves with the voice of love, pride, and self-assurance if we ever want others to speak to us that way. If our self-talk is holding us in guilt and shame for something that we did in our past, it is time to fight against that feeling of unforgiveness. Maybe we were promiscuous and we keep telling ourselves, "No good man will want me", or were incarcerated at some point and we are telling ourselves "I am an outcast", or perhaps we had children out of wedlock and now we are telling ourselves, "I have too much baggage". Whatever it might be that is making you believe that you are not worthy enough, it is time that you release that and forgive yourself, so that it no longer destroys your self-esteem.

Get ready to fight against that spirit of doubt that makes you second guess yourself, destroys your confidence, and stops you from being the person that you are created to be. Stop allowing past failures to dictate your future and damage your self-esteem. It does not matter if it is divorce, a lack of education, or a less than desirable family background. It is time to understand that your setbacks are not who you are. It is time allow the wisdom, strength, and knowledge that you gained from your experiences to be the things that boost your self-esteem and take you to the next level.

ADJUSTING MY SELF-CONCEPT

The problem that we often have with building our self-esteem is that we look outside of ourselves for validation. We look to other flawed individuals to bring value to our lives or we allow other flawed individuals to take value from our lives. We are getting our sense of self from the wrong sources. We often hear people say, "Only God can judge me" but then we listen to everyone but God on the verdict of who we are. We believe a relationship with something or someone else can bring us happiness, satisfaction, and meaning, so when that flawed individual tells us that we are too fat, or unattractive, or a failure we allow that to define us.

Our self-esteem issues are never about someone else, although they might seem that way. They are always about us. It is about where we put our trust, it's about the voices we listen to, and the words we decide to replay to ourselves about ourselves. We have to know the difference between the voice of truth and the voice of a liar. To find the truth I go back to the Bible. That alone tells me that all the hurtful and negative things that people have tried to make me believe that I am is a lie. I am not ugly, I am not stupid, I am not unlovable, worthless, hopeless, or senseless. Genesis tells me the truth about who I am and who I was created to be. "I am Godly", "I am royalty", "I am powerful", "I am loving and loveable", and "I am made in His image and likeness". That is the voice I listen to. Are you ready to listen also?

We must be ready to renew our self-concept in order to feel fulfilled in any relationship. In order to stop feeling inferior to others we must restore our dignity. If we are ready to feel deserving of a good and healthy partner, then we must reinstate our pride. We can no longer go on feeling like poor treatment from others is expected. We must raise our standards. In order to receive and give the love that we want and deserve we must learn to love ourselves first. Once we begin to adjust the way we see ourselves, change the way we talk to ourselves, and adjust the way we think of ourselves, we will be ready to take the next step.

Ready for Self-Love

In today's world of social media, relationship gurus, and life coaches, the term self-love is thrown around a lot. Though many of us use the term, I believe that the vast majority of us still have some confusion as to what the meaning and purpose of loving ourselves really is, and why it is so important to do so. Some of us have taken self-love and confused it with self-centeredness. We say that self-love is a time to put ourselves first – a time to be selfish. Some of us confuse it with self-conceit. We think its expression is taking selfies, posting ourselves on social media, and admiring how beautiful we think we are several times in a day, but that is not always self-love. The way that the world teaches self-love emphasizes a focus on *my* interests, my goals, my heart, my needs, etc.

The next thing that I am about to say might make

you put this book down or even throw it in the trash because it goes against what we have been getting taught by the world. It goes against our nature and forces us to look at self-love in a different way. The truth is, what we have been told self-love is will never get us ready for a relationship. That form of self-love will never prepare us to receive or give love to another individual. In fact, today's meaning of self-love does the exact opposite. It takes us in a different direction of relationship. It takes us down a road which makes us more self-absorbed, egotistical, and selfish. The concept of self-love is not wrong. We should have self-respect, we should go through self-discovery, self-actualization, and self-improve as I have written about. However, the way it has generally been taught and interpreted is what causes a problem for those of us desiring to be in relationship. Self-love was never meant to be to the end all, be all. Self-love was never meant to be the epitome of our love life.

"Love your neighbor as you love yourself." This scripture is where I get my understanding of self-love. I do not think that there is any recorded concept of self-love that is older than the one we find here. Through my study of this type of self-love, I have learned an important lesson: self-love is not about us.

Self-love is supposed to be a means to a bigger end. Self-love is meant to be stepping stone into a higher dimension of love. Self-love is a road we travel only to reach the destination of loving others. That is what self-love is all about: our neighbor.

If the end result of the self-love that we are practicing stops with us, then we have gotten it all wrong. If the self-love we are being taught has resulted in us having less patience with others but has expanded of our list of deal breakers and expectations for others there is a problem. If the self-love that we are ascribing to has caused us to be more self-seeking, self-serving, and self-promoting and less trusting, less connected, and less hopeful, then we have the entire concept of self-love backward. The self-love that we are being encouraged to follow today makes us turn away from relationship with others and it turns us toward a mindset where everything in our lives revolves around our wants and needs, and it stops there. The world's idea of self-love leaves out things such as: forgiveness, compromise, vulnerability, sharing, and sacrifice. These things are vital in any true relationship, and if the concept of self-love that you are following is not teaching you these qualities, then it is not getting you ready for a relationship.

Self-love only begins as an inside job, but it must

eventually make its way out to the people around us. It takes place in our hearts, souls, and minds. That is where self-love does the majority of its work. This is why it is so important to overcome past hurt, because hurt and hate cannot occupy the same space with healing and love. However, many of us try to make them roommates. We all have heard the saying, "hurt people hurt people", so we understand why hurt has to be evicted out of our heart in order for self-love to take residency. If we do not overcome the hurt and pain then the thing that we are calling self-love has an undertone of resentfulness, anger, and vengeance as we practice it. We have all seen people who try to prove to someone else that they love themselves, but true love needs no audience. Self-love does not have to prove anything to anyone. It just is.

The Bible speaks about the man that built his house on a sandy foundation and the man that built his house on a rocky foundation. Hurt, pain, anger, and resentfulness is a sandy foundation for self-love. If we are not healed and are just going through the motions of "dating ourselves", admiring ourselves, and focusing on our wants and needs, then every time we think we are ready for a relationship, the wind and rain that comes with every relationship will repeatedly knock down our self-esteem, self-image, self-worth, and what we thought was self-love. This is why self-love can only begin as an inside job but must eventually transition to the outside of loving others. That is the kind of love that has its foundation in God. That is the love that He strengthens. That is the love that will stand against any wind, rain, storm, and time.

We were never called to love ourselves just for the sake of loving ourselves. We want to build healthy and solid relationships. That is how we prepare ourselves to love the person that we will eventually meet when it is time for that deeper, more intimate relationship that we desire. Love others as you love yourself.

Ready for
Self-Worthiness

Self-worth is a term that is frequently used these days, but what does it really mean? How do we determine our worth? How do we build our worth? And how do make sure that people value us according to our worth? In our attempt to encourage and empower others we are constantly telling people to "know your worth", which is a great thing to say. Yes, we should know our worth. We should know how valuable we are; but do we?

Knowing our self-worth stops us from selling ourselves cheap. We will not trade our time, attention, and hearts for something that is not comparable in value. Although most of us have good intentions when we blurt out the phrase "know your worth", I feel that it is losing its meaning and power because it has become overly used but under-taught. I believe that an important step is being skipped in the "know your worth" movement. We tell people to know their worth without first understanding the scale that they are measuring their worth with. When we measure ourselves with a scale that is broken, uncalibrated, or with something that was never meant to measure self-worth in the first place, that is where the devaluing, mis-measuring, and misreading of one's worth comes in. So, how will we truly know our worth if that is the case? How will we ever reach our worth if that is the dilemma?

So I ask the question: who or what broke our self-worth scale? This takes me back to the question that God asked Adam and Eve when He found them hiding in the Garden of Eden. God asked, "Who told you were naked?" We need to ask ourselves, "Who told me I was worthless?", "Who said that I would never amount to anything?", and "Who conditioned me to think that I was not good enough?" So many of us have been measuring ourselves with the words, memories, and experiences that were meant to break us. We have been finding our value in lies, insults, put downs, and the beat downs that we endured throughout life. Maybe it is the abandonment, the abuse and neglect, or poverty and misfortune we suffered that drove us to the conclusion that we must be worthless and unworthy. The point that I am trying to make is that

that is a broken scale and we will continue to feel unworthy if we continue to use it. We will never feel that we deserve good things if we use a rating scale that is designed to tell us that we are less than, subordinate, and worthless.

If you have children, you can probably remember when they became obsessed with their height and they wanted you to measure them every day to see if they grew taller than three feet. There were days that they wanted to return the favor and measure you. But the highest they could reach with their measuring tape is your shoulder because you were so much taller than them. How accurate would their reading be? How much of you would they be disregarding simply because they are too small to measure how big you really are? This is what happens when we measure ourselves with the inaccurate scale that others try to use on us. This is the method used by an abuser, a perpetrator, and someone that feels worthless themselves. They try to chop us down to their size. They try to make us believe that we are small, when we are actually giants. They want us to believe that we are weak when we are actually strong. They attempt to make us think that we are unlovable, when the greatest love known to mankind has already been given to us. We help them by believing it. We must adjust our scale or throw it away if it is a broken one. We cannot continue to measure ourselves with a scale that was created to be used against us, because it will never tell us what we are really worth.

When we are not using a broken scale, we are often using the wrong scale to measure our worth. We use our physical appearance to measure our worth, or we might use the likes and loves on social media, or we look for self-worth in the car we drive, the money we make, the degrees we have, or the relationship that we are in. If this is the case, there is no wonder why we do not know our worth, because these type of things were never meant to measure it. When we find our worth in the superficial and temporary things of this world we will always feel worthless because those things do not hold their value. They are constantly changing, and are relative. They are based on other people's preference and opinions, not fact. If we find ourselves measuring our value by the car we drive, we must realize that our car depreciates in value the second it is driven off the lot, along with our feelings of self-worth attached to it. So what do we end up doing? We run back to the dealership every time the car loses its shine because it feels like we have lost ours. Material items are supposed to be used for measuring net worth not self-worth.

Maybe we are the type that measure our worth by what see in our social media feed, something else that holds no value. Every time we do not get enough likes, every time we compare ourselves to the picture of an airbrushed, photo-shopped Instagram model that has 10k more hearts than us and realize that we look nothing like that, what happens to our feelings of self-worth? We also measure our worth by the type relationship we are in, or the fact that we are in or not in one. Relationships are up and down. They have good times and horrible times. We can be in one today and out of it tomorrow. How do you think our feelings of self-worth are affected if we attach them to something so inconsistent? Some of us are terrified of being alone and depressed by the thought of being single. We look for our self-worth from people and things outside of self, and this is why we never feel complete. Material items, people's opinions, and not even a relationship can ever complete us. We are using the wrong scale.

Years ago the American dollar was backed by gold and silver. That is what made it valuable. That is what made it worth something. We could actually measure gold and find the equivalent dollar amount. Today it is not – we can no longer trade money for gold. We can only trade money for the goods and services it can buy. This is how things like cryptocurrency have found a way into the economy. But I use this only as an example to illustrate how we are backed not by gold, but by the One whose streets are paved with gold. The One whose measuring scale is never broken or inaccurate. Our self-worth is not determined by our family, friends, possessions, or even ourselves. Our value is determined by God. God has given us our gifts and talents. He is the only one that can tell us who we are and what we will be, and it is up to us to make sure that these gifts and talents do not go to waste. To be ready for a relationship, we have to understand where to go to measure our self-worth. Just to give you an idea of what you are worth and how valuable you are I will leave you with this:

There was a king that ruled over a kingdom. This king had one beloved child. This child meant the world to him. So much so that they were like one person. There came a time when his kingdom was in grave danger and faced total destruction. The only way to save it was for the king to give up his only beloved son as a sacrifice. Because the people of his kingdom were so valuable to him, and because his kingdom was worth so much, he sacrificed his only son to save the kingdom. If you are familiar with the story then you know that I am speaking about

God as that King, Jesus as that Son, and you are that kingdom. That is how valuable and worthy you are. Know your worth.

4. Mutuality Mind-Set

If we look up the meaning of the word mutual, we will find this definition: relating to each other, things held in common; shared experience, respect to the other; reciprocal. A mutuality mindset is all about transforming our minds and lives to be in true relationship with someone else. It is learning to be in a partnership. Mutuality mindset is the idea that combining my world with someone else's world will lead to the creation of a better world together. Having a mutuality mindset means that we trade in our pride of independence for reliance on interdependence. Somewhere along the line, we began to misinterpret independence; as a result, relationships began to die. When we develop a mutuality mindset we begin to understand that independence frees us of the control from others, but independence was never meant to stop us from connecting with others. We still need one another.

Men need women and women need men. With a mutuality mindset we learn to value the differences that we bring to the table, as opposed to disliking and judging each other because of those differences. We learn that we have to take the feelings, thoughts, habits, and everything else that a person brings into consideration. It is no longer about me or you: it is about us. A mutuality mindset is needed in order to experience a healthy exchange of feelings. It is essential in order to accomplish a positive transfer and countertransference of ideas. To be ready for a relationship means we must be ready for a mutuality mindset.

Now, there is a lot of irony in getting ourselves ready for a mutuality mindset. Because after our healing takes place, when finding our self-worth is accomplished, and when we become confident and committed in our relationship with God, some of our ambition for mutuality in a relationship gets lost. Our preparation for a relationship can actually bring us to a point where we begin to question if we even have the desire to be in one. After experiencing the peace and joy of God, conquering our fears, and finding our purpose in life, letting another person into our world can be scary. It can feel like an inconvenience, and it can feel like a step backward in some cases. As much as we hate to admit it, we can become selfish. We can become very possessive with our time. We can become extremely protective of our space. It becomes difficult to open up our lives, hearts, or even our schedules to fit someone else in. We hit a certain sweet spot in our lives and we do not want it to be derailed by the struggles that a relationship can bring. We have found peace, purpose, and pleasure in ourselves. The "me" mindset has shown good results so getting back to the "we" mindset can be a challenge.

If we chose to be honest with ourselves again, we will admit that deep down inside, most of us still really want to be in a good relationship. Even if that craving has been buried under all the new goals we are pursuing. The desire might have gotten hidden behind our new found purpose in life. The yearning for a relationship might have even been put on the back burner while going to the gym, getting that degree, going to Bible study, starting that business, or writing that book was moved to the front. The truth is, that desire is still there. We still want to experience true love with another individual. We still want to be cared for and supported when we are going through tough times. We want someone special to celebrate our accomplishments with. We still want date night. We want commitment and we want someone to hold and to be affectionate with.

So, how do we overcome this selfishness? How do we move to the next level of relationship readiness, where we can open up our lives, and make ourselves emotionally, physically, and spiritually available to someone again? How do we transition from thinking "me" to thinking "we"? We must develop a mutuality mindset.

This might seem like common sense when we are talking about relationships, but it can be difficult to put into practice for a lot of us. Previously I mentioned that we like to create lists. The top five must have's list. The deal breakers list. The must nots list. I believe that subconsciously a lot of this is done as a protective measure. It is a way of keeping people out and keeping our world under our control as much as we possibly can. We fail to see how these things fight against developing a mutuality mindset.

I have been at this point where having a mutuality mindset was a struggle. Especially after I had reached a certain stage in life and certain things were established. Opening up my world was a huge challenge for me. There were things about myself that needed to be changed in order for me to become more prepared to open up my life and my heart. To share my world, I needed to focus on some key areas that helped me create that mutuality mindset, and that is what this section will be discussing.

Mutual Integration

A lot of the concepts that are explored in this book are probably done best independently: getting to know ourselves, overcoming past pain, and building a stronger relationship with God. Though we can receive outside help with all of these things, the main work requires alone time, solitude, and meditation. Much of it calls for us to find a quiet space and getting in seclusion to really do some self-examination and healing. Developing a mutual mindset is different. This is something that we cannot do alone. We have to come out of isolation. We must abandon some privacy. We have to interact with others in order to put a mutuality mindset into practice. Allow me to apologize to all those that consider themselves introverts. I am sure that you were comfortable with the alone time, but this integration that must be done also includes us.

Mutual integration means we can no longer totally separate ourselves. It takes some inclusion. It requires us to interact, fellowship, mix and mingle with others. For one, we cannot expect to be on the same page with others if we do not socialize enough and find out what page they are on. It takes us leaving the comfort zone of our homes, or jobs, or friends, and actually meeting people, talking to people, and exchanging ideas, interests, and passions with others. We cannot find mutuality in seclusion and confinement. We can no longer use God as the scapegoat. Waiting for God does not mean we do nothing. We must add some type of work to our faith, and the least that we can do is to put ourselves in a position where finding mutuality with someone is possible.

In no other area of lives do we expect God to do all of the work like we do when it comes to dating and relationships. When we are looking for a job, we pray and fill out applications and go on interviews. When we are looking for a house, we pray and find a realtor and go to open house viewings. When we become sick, we pray and find a way to get better by seeing our doctor or getting some cold medicine. Why is it that when it comes to dating and relationships so many of us pray and sit home, or just go back and forth to work, or to church, or overcompensate in some other area of life as a way to intentionally avoid social interaction? We do this as if God is going to drop someone at our doorstep. We can trust that God will always do His part, but there is a part that we also have to play. We must integrate ourselves with others in order to create a mutuality mindset, and find mutuality.

Many times people say that they will leave it in God's hands when the truth is, we do not trust ourselves to make the right choice. We do not trust our own judgement, so we think that relinquishing all responsibility is the answer. However I can guarantee that after we have done the work of self-awareness, after we have self-actualized, after we have developed true self-love, we will no longer distrust our ability to choose. We will have established our standards and those standards will align with what our needs truly are, and what God has already told us He wants.

Integrating in order to have a mutuality mindset does not only mean that we make ourselves physically available, where we just show up (but it's a start). We also have to make ourselves emotionally and mentally available. This is why it is so important to go through that healing process, because if one brings baggage from the past it makes it extremely difficult or almost impossible to be present on an emotional or mental level with someone that you might meet in the future. We are distracted. The preoccupation with hurt, fear, and anxiety stops us from being mentally and emotionally accessible. The only way a relationship can build is if there are two people putting their hearts into it. It takes the mutual integration of trust, support, nurturing, and communication in order for it work. For some, this can be frightening, but we must take the risk of becoming reachable if we want to get the reward of a relationship. We have to sow if we want to reap. We must put in if we want to get something out. This is a universal principle that we cannot avoid. In order to receive that love and loyalty that we desire in a relationship, we have to be emotionally available so that mutual exchange can happen.

We have to integrate ourselves mentally, which takes us being in the moment. A lot of times it is hard to get on the same page with someone because we do not know how to get out of our own heads and just be present. We get distracted by our own thoughts. We get caught in worrying about the events of tomorrow and things of yesterday, which takes us away from enjoying today. We meet an individual and our first concerns are things that could go wrong in the future, or if they are untrustworthy like the ones from your past. We get so consumed by our own thoughts that they hinder us from mentally integrating ourselves in the here and now. At times those fearful thoughts and anxious feelings stop us from even attempting to explore the possibility that there might be compatibility with someone. We allow our fear, hurt, anger, or self-sabotaging to control our behavior and destroy things before they even begin.

When it is not fearful thoughts keeping our minds cluttered, they are crammed with thoughts about work, household duties, children, and goals. In order to be mutually integrated there are times when we even have to clear our minds of the everyday rigmarole in order to be mentally engaged with someone else.

In no way I am saying that one should totally tear down their protective wall, but we must lower it to an appropriate height and at an appropriate time in order to make a connection. Something as simple as a smile, or as easy as a response when you are greeted is a good place to start. Mutual integration is the first step to building a mutual mindset. You have done the inner work. You have done the intangible work with God. Now it is time to do the integration work.

Mutual Vulnerability

Learning to be vulnerable is a major piece in developing a mutuality mindset. When we decide to be vulnerable we are deciding to lower our defenses. We are breaking down the walls. We are removing the barriers that keep our world separated from others. Experiencing true love and a mutual vulnerability goes hand in hand because we must be willing to reveal our needs, our desires, our shortcomings, and insecurities to others in order to accomplish this. Vulnerability provides others with opportunity to meet our true self. It gives them the chance cover us in areas we are broken, love us in spite of our quirks, and walk with us through our fears. That is love.

A major problem in relationships today is that we enter into them with unrealistic expectations. We expect our mates to meet a need that we were never vulnerable enough to share with them. We expect to draw closer to them and for them to draw closer to us, even when we do not learn how to loosen our grip on the need to protect ourselves, and break down the wall that impedes closeness. Mutual vulnerability requires us to release the fear of showing someone who we really are.

We can only see eye to eye with someone by allowing them to look deep into our eyes and see the inner parts of us. Vulnerability is the lifeline to experiencing true love and intimacy, and it is the key to having a relationship that is built on mutuality.

One of the biggest things that hinders our ability to be vulnerable is our ability to trust. Ironically, there is only one way to overcome those trust issues, and it lies in our willingness to be vulnerable. What I mean is, I can only build trust with someone if I let down my guard and open my heart so that they have an opportunity to get close enough to prove that they are trustworthy. If I continue to build barriers between myself and others, I will be stuck in a cycle of mistrust and doubt. Of course we must use our discernment when choosing who to trust. We also must use our discernment to understand the difference between when our hesitancy to trust is due to the character of that individual, or if it comes from issues that we carry around from past experiences. We then have to become courageous enough to charter territory that makes us feel a little uncomfortable and insecure. Many times we project our own insecurities onto our partner, in attempt to make it seem like it is a flaw in them which keeps us from being vulnerable, and that destroys relationships.

For example, someone would say, "If I tell my partner about my embarrassing past I am afraid that they will judge me or use it against me in the future". Do you see how this person has taken the insecurities of their past and turned it into a flaw of being judgmental and vengeful in their partner? What they are really doing is creating an excuse for why they choose not to be vulnerable. Now they have lost out on an opportunity to build intimacy, trust, and support in their relationship.

It is important to realize that there will not be a mutual exchange of respect, empathy, and love if we cannot open ourselves up to give and receive it. When we allow others to see who we really are and where we come from, it builds a natural closeness, if we are dealing with the right person. When we make ourselves accessible, that builds an instant bond, and that bond forces us to think more of "we" and less of "me". That is the core of mutuality. I had to learn that in order to have the reciprocity that comes with a mutual mindset I could not be afraid to reveal my weaknesses, my strengths, my heart, my struggles, or my pain. We cannot have the expectation of openness if we are not able to be open.

I have to push this idea of vulnerability because it truly is the source of any genuine relationship. If someone feels that they do not know who we are, or if we come across as if we are hiding behind a persona, or keeping others at arm's length, we will be missing out on creating great connections with other people.

I know that being emotionally available and vulnerable is scary. Some of us have tried it in the past and as a result we were left wounded, hurt, and broken. That level of pain and disappointment we experienced has actually made some of us associate heartache with relationship. In our minds, love and pain are synonymous, so in order to protect our hearts, we choose to never be vulnerable again. What we fail to realize is that the wall that we build to keep us from meeting someone similar to the person that hurt and violated our vulnerability, is the same wall that stops us from meeting the right one: someone that would cover us, love us, and protect our vulnerability. Our walls do not discriminate on who they keep out or let in. They just keep everyone out.

Many of us want to be vulnerable but don't know how to because fear, pain, and trauma stops us. Here is the secret to how to be more accessible and open: become more accessible and open again. That is it. There is no way around it. It is very similar to teaching a child how to ride a bike. A child will never learn how to ride until they get exposed to what they fear and has the potential to hurt them, and that is falling. Eventually the training wheels must come off, the parent must let go of the handlebars, and the child must take the chance of falling in order to learn how to ride. Now, there are things that are put in place to soften the fall and lower the chance of injury. She is strapped with her knee and elbow pads, she has on a helmet, and she might even have in a mouthpiece. Just in case she does fall, she will have the ability to get back up. For those of us who hesitate with being vulnerable because we fear falling, we have to put on similar protective equipment to decrease the injury and potential for long lasting pain. The self-acceptance work that we did is our helmet, the self-discovery work that went through are our kneepads, the self-esteem we have built are our elbow pads, and the self-worth that we realized is our mouthpiece. All that work that we have done protects us from the pain of a fall when we decide to be vulnerable. When we have built ourselves up and if someone attempts to take advantage of our openness we will be able to withstand it because we know who we are. If someone tries to use our soft spots and sensitivities against us, it will not work because we already have built up our self-esteem. We have discovered and accepted ourselves so there is nothing someone else can say or do to affect that now. Even if we fall, we will bounce right back up. It will be easier to heal from simple flesh wound that someone tries to create, because we took out the time to become internally healthy before we entered into the relationship. It will no longer feel like there are disappointments stacked on top disappointments, or hurt piled over more hurt. We will deal with that isolated incident without generalizing it or internalizing it, which makes a fall easier to bounce back from.

Vulnerability is only scary when we do not know who we are as a person. You will discover that it is much easier showing others who you are when you have fully embraced yourself. We are terrorized by the thought of opening up our hearts when we have not healed from past hurt, but we will learn that when we have healed from our past we are more courageous to walk toward our future.

In order to become vulnerable, we also have to get

over the idea that we have to be perfect, and we have to overcome the belief that others are better than us in some way. We live in an era where people like to show their highlights and hide their hard times. On social media we only post pictures when we are on vacation, out having fun with friends, when we just left the salon or barber shop, or to show our latest accomplishments. How many times do you see someone post a picture of themselves when they first wake up in morning? People will show pictures of their money but not their bills. God forbid they put up a picture of when they are having a terrible hair day.

There is this need to appear perfect to the world. This stops all of us from being vulnerable. The fear of being judged or looked at as weak prevents us from revealing that we have bad times as well as good times. We are constantly watching others live their best lives, and we begin to feel like everyone's life is better than ours. As a result, we go into a deeper hiding, we put on a bigger mask, we develop a stronger complex, and we avoid being vulnerable. We have to change our perspective on what vulnerability is. Having the courage to show that you are not perfect is actually very powerful. If you do not believe me, ask the person that gathered the strength to overcome an alcohol addiction only because they kept going to AA meetings where people were sharing their stories, talking about their struggles, pain, addictions, and accomplishments. Or speak to the person that went through therapy and finally had a breakthrough because they became vulnerable and were able to talk about their trauma. We can walk into a church and find someone that was encouraged to face their issues after hearing the testimony of the pastor or another member of the congregation. Vulnerability is not only powerful for the person that is being open but it helps others around them. It is a strength. The ability to display a full scope of emotions takes vulnerability. To cry, laugh, smile, or show disappointment and excitement is powerful.

Just as every cigarette pack has a warning label, I would like to leave you with a warning about vulnerability. Vulnerability is the ability to display a "full scope" of emotion. Do not be misled into thinking that because someone is able to share all of their pain, hurt, and disappointments in life that it always means that they have a mutuality mindset. Some could just be looking for sympathy and hoping to receive help, but not willing to give help. Others might be looking for someone to dump their problems on but never looking to help someone else with their challenges. Be careful not to mistake sharing common pain with someone as being vulnerable with someone. There is a thing called "shared trauma" which also bonds people, but it does not automatically translate to vulnerability and mutuality. There are times when it can translate to enabling and one-sided relationships. It can also lead to being used for your nurturing and caring nature. Genuine vulnerability and openness does not look to take advantage or others. The purpose of sharing in mutuality is not to seek sympathy but to seek intimacy.

Mutual Compromise

As I examined this concept called compromise, it became clear that the overall consensus was that a lot people are against it. A great amount of the material that I came across declared: "NEVER COMPROMISE ON WHAT YOU WANT!"," NEVER GIVE IN!", and "NEVER SETTLE!". The idea that we should have things our way is really pushed in this society. There exists an unspoken belief that compromise means surrender. This point that I will be making about developing a mutual mindset through compromising may be a hard concept to embrace in such a self-centered, narcissistic, never-give-in culture.

Compromise is the foundation of having a mutuality mindset, which I will explain later. But to understand that explanation we must first understand something about having a mutual mindset. Do not be bamboozled into believing that a mutual mindset means that we find this organic, magical connection with another person, where we think alike, finish each other's sentences, and share the same birthday. Developing a mutuality mindset does not mean that we find this undeniable chemistry with someone whose soul links with ours, and the heavens open up and God says in a thundering voice, "This is the one". Because having a mutuality mindset is not some magical mystical majestic occurrence, this is where the readiness for compromise comes in. Being ready for a mutuality mindset means that we have to be ready to compromise. Yes, compromise. Just the mention of the word lets you know that things will not always be smooth and agreeable, decisions will not always go your way, and that we will not think exactly alike or be in full agreement with everything our mate says or believes. This is where the rubber meets the road in most relationships; facing the reality that most of the time we will have to compromise in order to get on the same page.

What is compromise and why is it needed in order to have a mutuality mindset? Compromise is putting forth the effort to reach an agreement, where both parties make adjustments to their positions for the overall benefit of the relationship and the achievement of a shared goal. For instance, you and a friend decided that you both want to grab a bite to eat and to enjoy some activities. The problem is, your friend wants Chinese food and you want a burger, and your friend wants to go to the mall afterward, but you would rather go for a nature walk in the park. You both share the common goal of eating and an activity, but your positions on the best and most desirable way to achieve that goal differ. What would be a good compromise in this situation? Since you want to eat two different things and want to participate in two different activities, it would be a good compromise to split it right down the middle. The two of you can have Chinese for dinner then take a walk in the park, or you can have a hamburger and then go to the mall. This scenario is quite simple to figure out on paper, but it can be much more difficult in real life when we consider people's emotions, their attachment to what they want, and their beliefs regarding what the better option is. These things make compromise and having a mutuality mindset challenging for many.

One of the things that gets in the way of our ability to compromise is our pride. The belief that we know best and we have the only solution to any given issue. We can become very self-righteous about how things should go. Many of us secretly believe that we are smarter, wiser, and know more than our counterpart and that belief will always get in the way of our ability to compromise. We dig our heels in the sand, become stiff in our position, and before you know it something as trivial as where to spend the holidays turns into World War III.

As we further explore the idea of having a mutual mindset and the importance of compromise, we must highlight two of most important characteristics that we have to develop in order to compromise and those are: respect and humility.

We must learn to raise our level of respect and appreciation for others and their opinions. We must learn to humble ourselves and stop believing that we have the only answer. We must see value in the choices that other people make, even if it is not a choice that we would personally make. I was once taught that we have to view our mate as competent and capable in order to have respect and appreciation for them and their views. Our willingness or unwillingness to compromise is a perfect way to examine if we view our mate competent and capable. If we do not, I can be sure that compromise will be a challenge in our relationship. We have to be more open and willing to adjust our own desires. We must respect the fact that people are individuals, and that what they want is important to them. What they desire makes them happy and comfortable, and we have to respect that even if it is not something that makes us totally happy. It is so important to start compromising when making decisions on trivial things such as: what to eat, what movies to watch, or what road will get us to our destination fastest – the smaller things that we debate about. In order to be a better compromiser we can choose to decide that there is no ideal option in many cases. They are both preferences, which does not make one better or worse than the other. As a relationship advances and develops into something bigger, the things that we have to compromise on also get bigger. The good thing is that we have practiced compromising on the small things which will make compromising on the big things a little less difficult.

I have seen beautiful relationships end because the couple refused to compromise. I have seen a thirty-year marriage destroyed in divorce court because they were not willing to practice a little give and take in their relationship. The failure to compromise is poison to any relationship. You might be the one that argues better, presents your evidence clearer, or is just willing to fight longer and dirtier, beating your mate into submission, which leads to you getting your way most of the time. However, while you are enjoying the spoils of your victory, your partner is growing more resentful by the day. Your mate is feeling more controlled, more frustrated, more devalued, and more ready to leave the relationship. Compromise is key to developing a mutuality mindset and getting you ready to be the person that someone else will want to stay in a relationship with.

Do not get me wrong: there are certain things that we should not compromise on. Things like our morals, values, and beliefs. As long as those morals and values are grounded in righteousness and a positive nature, there should be no compromise on that. If someone is asking you to compromise on the things that makes you the person that you are, or the principles that govern the way you live, you might want to question if this is the right individual for you.

I believe that we should never settle but always compromise. Make sure that things are fair when trying to reach an agreement, even if it means you get the short end of the stick this time, but next time you get the longer end. One method I often try when compromising is a rating scale. I ask myself, "On a scale of 1 to 10, 10 being very important and 1 being insignificant, how important is this thing that I want versus the thing she wants to happen?" If it ranks low on my rating scale, then I have no problem letting go or adjusting on what I wanted. In other words, pick your battles. No one wants to be in relationship where everything feels like a tug of war. Being ready for a relationship means being ready for compromise. Any good partnership takes a healthy level of give and take in order to keep each other happy and satisfied with the arrangement. Relationships are no different.

Mutual Sacrifice

Sacrifice and compromise might seem closely related but they are actually distant cousins. As we continue our discussion of this notion of getting into a mutuality mindset, we will see that the willingness and readiness to make sacrifices is a key ingredient to any sustainable relationship. Sacrifice is one of the things which require us to give without taking. It requires us to pour out without necessarily getting poured back into. Sacrifice is doing something for someone else without expecting an immediate return on your investment. It is done simply out of love, care, concern, and the kindness of our hearts. Sacrifice is a true test of our faith because we are letting go of something in hopes that it will benefit a greater good, and in this case the greater good would be the strengthening of the relationship. In order to be ready for a relationship, we must be ready to make sacrifices.

There are a lot of benefits and opportunities in

singleness. There is the freedom to do what we want, when we want, without informing someone or getting permission or considering another person's input. In singleness we have the advantage of being selfish with our time, finances, and space if we choose to. If we want to stay at home on the weekend alone, we can. There is no one there pressuring us to spend quality time with them. If we want to go out with the girls or guys, we do not have to consider what another person's plans are for that night. We can just go. So when we say that we are ready for a relationship we have to realize that we are saying that we are ready to sacrifice some of the benefits that singleness brings.

There are so many people that want to be in a relationship but still want to live the single life at the same time. That is a formula that never works. Certain benefits of being single must be sacrificed if we want to be in a successful relationship. I have many friends that have went on to get married. These friends and I use to go out every weekend, party, and have fun. We would stumble into the house anytime that we pleased because we were single at the time. Can you imagine if the ones that are now married did not sacrifice their weekends of fun with their friends? If they still chose to stumble into the house anytime that they wanted, how would that affect their marriage?

Sacrifice is hard, because it is only a sacrifice if we are letting go of something that is important to us. The challenge with today's single is that we believe that our happiness is the most important thing in the world. The idea of temporarily sacrificing happiness to achieve a bigger purpose is inconceivable these days. But here is a news flash: "relationships will not always make us happy". There are times when we will have to go against the emotion of happiness, sacrifice a joyful feeling, and fight through the hard times that come with relationships. We have to go against our preference when compromising, expose ourselves to hurt emotions when being vulnerable, and navigate disagreements when we communicate our truth. We must get out of the fantasy that a relationship should always feel like cotton candy and rainbows. It takes sacrifice, and sacrifice never feels comfortable, but if we want to develop a mutuality mindset we have to believe that it will be worth it. The question is, are we ready to make sacrifices? If not, then we have to ask ourselves, are we really ready for a relationship?

The experience of being with someone that you are willing to make sacrifices for and they are willing to make sacrifices for you is one of the most beautiful things that we can ever experience in the world. That means you have someone that will put your needs before their wants. The two of you serve each other, support each other, and pour into each other. Can you imagine having someone in your life that will give up things that they desire to help you become the best version of you, and the reason they are willing to put their personal preferences to the side is because they feel that your elevation is their elevation? You being happy is what make them happy, and your accomplishment is not only a reflection of them, but they are a part of it. That is why we sacrifice for someone else. It is an act of intimacy. It unites us. It is a display of love. If you want to know if you are ready to be in a relationship with someone, check to see how much you are willing to sacrifice for them and that will tell you all that you need to know.

By this point in the book I do not have to tell you that we are referring to a sacrifice that is healthy and reciprocal. If your first thought when you read this is, "I sacrificed before and they took advantage of me – I'll never do it again", go back to the beginning of the book and focus on healing because you are not ready for a mutuality mindset yet. You are still hurt. However if you are ready for it, I ask that you embrace this idea of sacrifice, put it in practice, and I guarantee you will be better as a result of it.

Mutual Support

If I asked the question, "What are you looking for in a mate?" There is no doubt that I would get some variation of the following responses: "I want someone that compliments me"; "I want someone that supports me"; or "I want someone that has my best interests at heart". These are all things most of us want right? It does not sound unreasonable. We have busy lives. We have career goals, fitness goals, family goals, good times and bad times. It makes sense to want someone who supports what we are doing and what we are going through. Because we are so ambitious, our plates are so full, and we go through so much we can get caught up in the desire of being supported with our stuff. We can easily forget the importance reciprocity, supporting others, complimenting others, or having others' best interests at heart. We all love the feeling of receiving support, but we cannot neglect the giving part.

Developing a sense of mutual support is a huge part of having a mutuality mindset.

We have grown more narcissistic as a society. There is an emphasis on self. We hold independence in such high esteem and we only see the value of connecting with others if we are able to get something out of the deal, something that pushes us toward our goals and dreams. This mindset might be great for advancing in the business world, and it might help with the goal of climbing the corporate ladder, but self-centeredness, narcissistic behavior, and self-absorption will put a relationship on death row.

I held a discussion with a young lady who was struggling with moving a dating situation to the next level of being in a committed relationship with someone. She described her life as being extremely busy. She was a businesswoman that had very little time. She explained that she needed a man that was supportive of her lifestyle and all that she did, one who was able to "get in where he fit in" when she had time. Before she even finished, I could see one of the major problems, just as you probably can.

Relationships cannot be all about us or they will always fail. We must be willing and able to give as much support as we are expecting. We must invest time in each other, we must pour into each other, and we must uplift, encourage, and be there for each other. No one wants to be in a relationship with an energy vampire. An energy vampire is someone who sucks their mate dry of energy in order to keep themselves going, keep themselves motivated, and keep themselves energized in order give themselves to the world, then they come home to give their mate the scraps. Mutual support means that we give our mate just much as they give us. We boost them as highly as they lift us. A mutual submission to the mission of each other is needed in order for us to truly be ready for a relationship.

Mutual Sexuality

Sexuality is a major part of every romantic relationship. As we continue on this path toward developing a mutuality mindset, we must understand that the need to be on the same page sexually with our mate is as important, if not more important than anything else. Whether we are practicing abstinence or are sexually active, if we are holding onto our virginity or we are adventurous with our bodies, a mutual understanding of each other's preferences, needs, and sexual boundaries will only benefit our relational growth. Our ability and willingness to be sexual with each other encompasses many things. There are levels and layers to it. There is an appropriate time and an appropriate way for each layer of our sexuality to be revealed as a relationship develops. To prevent it from being the thing that makes or breaks our relationship, there must be a mutual agreement on how our sexuality is expressed, what it means to each individual, and the importance of sexuality in our relationships.

I could have called this section mutual intimacy, but I wanted to be sure that it would not be confused with everything else that we have previously discussed. A lot of things fall under the umbrella of intimacy, and sexuality is one form of intimacy that deserves to be addressed directly. When I speak about our sexuality I am not just talking about the act of sexual intercourse. Mutual sexuality involves understanding each other's sexual identity. Mutual sexuality means that we learn about each other's sexual history. Mutual sexuality requires us to communicate our sexual traumas and dysfunctions. And of course it means that we become interested in each other's sexual pleasures and desires.

I often say, in order to be in a healthy relationship you must be a healthy individual. I can also say, in order to be in a healthy relationship you must have a healthy sex life. That does not mean that you must have sex three times a day. What I mean by a healthy sex life is that you and your mate must practice the same habits and behaviors with your sexuality that you would practice with any other aspect of your relationship if you want it to be healthy. We must be honest. We have to be transparent. We should be nonjudgmental. We must be fair, and we cannot manipulate, use, or abuse others in any sexual way. That is a healthy sex life and sexual mutuality.

Sexuality and sex can be a very touchy subject for so many of us, because chances are we were never taught how to have a healthy conversation about it. If you are like me, sex was briefly covered in health class, where the extent of our sex education was when we were taught how to put a condom on a cucumber. Or you were scared straight and traumatized when your biology teacher made your class watch *The Miracle of Childbirth*. This undoubtedly left a whole lot of questions unanswered. Some of us only learned about sex through the perspective of the religious authorities in our lives, which do not always give us a full teaching and understanding of sexuality. A majority of us learned about sex by looking at pornographic magazines and movies, or listening to friends who did not know too much more than us. My point is, there has been a lack of accurate and healthy discussion about sexuality and sex, and the impact is seen in the taboo way we deal with this topic in our relationships today. With developing a mutuality mindset about our sexuality, we must learn to move past the censorships, see through the condemnation, and give each other the freedom to be who we truly are.

In mutual sexuality we are learning to let go and overcome the shame, guilt, and blame that often comes with it. The goal is to have a mutual understanding of where each other stands. We must grow to a point where we are able to talk about sexual abuse from our past, how we healed from it, and/or the impact it has on the way we function in the present. We want to be able to discuss any sexual identity challenges that we might have had or are still having. Sexual mutuality means that we have to be transparent with our sexual urges or even sexual strangeness. Sexual mutuality means that we are able to share our need for affection and closeness. It also means that we can communicate why intimacy and displays of sexual affection might make you uncomfortable. We want to feel like our mindset when it comes to sexuality is accepted, embraced, mutual, and that we are on one accord.

Mutual Communication

Communication usually ranks pretty high on most people's list as an element to a successful relationship. Because of this, I felt that it was only right to round up this section on developing a mutuality mindset with a discussion of the need for mutual communication. Communication is the lifeline of any relationship. Without effective communication it is impossible to be on the same page. The main ingredients of everything that has been discussed in this chapter are part of communication: integration, vulnerability, compromise, sacrifice, support, and sexuality. None of these can be possible or complete without communication. Let us take a look at what a relationship is, and why communication is so important in getting to that "us" mindset that we have been exploring.

In a relationship we have two people, born and raised by different parents, separate family cultures, and maybe even contrasting ethnic backgrounds. Two people that have had different life experiences, and even if they grew up in similar circumstances the way they have processed those events are distinct to them. One is a man and one is a woman. The way they were conditioned to view the world was not consistently the same. Now they want to get together and live as one in harmony for the rest of their lives. How is this possible? How can they get to the point when they begin to think "we" when they are so different? How can two people with foreign backgrounds, unfamiliar behaviors, and specific idiosyncrasies create a mutuality mindset? Communication is the key. Without it, it is impossible to have unity and understanding between two people.

In order to form a mutuality mindset, we must be open to listening, understanding, and learning the voice and heart of another individual. Those three components are vital to effective communication. Communication is more intimate than sex. I once heard intimacy explained in a very profound way: intimacy can be translated as "into me see". There is only one pathway to seeing the very soul of another person, and that is through communication. We can have sex with someone and never get to know them, we can live with someone for years and never understand them, and we could have grown up in the same neighborhood with someone and still not know who they truly are, but communication lets us into the world and mind of our partner like nothing else does.

If we are trying to transition from the me mentality to the we mentality, we must learn to listen to others. We must seek to understand others. We must speak in love and in truth, and we have to become humble enough to learn from someone else. We have to possess the desire to see who the other person really is, and we have to allow them to see the true us. I know this is easier said than done. We have all probably tried to do these things that I have mentioned in the past and received the short end of the stick. But the truth is, if we ever want to be ready for a relationship, there is no other way. This is the only path. We will have to get up from the dirt and begin to brush off the hurt, pain, and disappointment, and try again, and again, and maybe again.

LISTENING IN COMMUNICATION

We often believe that talking is communicating,

when the truth is that talking is only one method of communication. It is only one piece of a much bigger puzzle. Talking is not even the most important piece in that puzzle of communication. Our ability to be a good listener has been proven to be a far more vital part of effective communication than speaking, yet it is the most underutilized part. Our inability to listen properly and attentively could be the biggest barrier to us developing a mutuality mindset. It is extremely hard to function as partners if one person does not listen to the other's needs. It is almost impossible for two people to be in agreement if all one hears is their own perspective, feelings, and experience. Furthermore, the inability to listen with a keen ear is what makes people miss red flags and overlook inconsistencies in others. Listening not only helps us to be on the same page with someone; it also helps us in knowing if we should be reading an entirely different book.

In the psychology world there is a communication technique that is used called reflective listening. With reflective listening the intent is to listen to gain clarity and understanding. As two people communicate, one will listen observantly in silence, allowing the other to finish their thoughts or statement. The listener will then paraphrase what they believed was said by the speaker for confirmation of understanding. The speaker will either correct or confirm what was heard and understood by the listener. This is a very basic and very effective communication technique.

I have always been amused by the irony of the spelling of the words "listen" and "silent", because both words are spelled with the exact same letters, and the two words also go hand in hand. One cannot be accomplished without the other. Often when two people are attempting to communicate one only stays silent long enough to think of a response, defend their argument, or come up with an insult, or because they have checked out from the conversation.

Those with a mutuality mindset listen with a specific objective, which is different from the vast majority of people. They listen to identify the commonalities. They listen for areas where there is synergy. They listen for the foundational things that a relationship can be built on. They do not allow their fear and anxiety to take over the dialogue. There are others who strictly focus on the things that they do not agree with. They search for things that they do not have in common with others. From my experience, this occurs with individuals that need to heal. Someone that is still dealing with unresolved hurt and lingering anger. Pain usually shows its face in the way they hear, listen, and process what is said. Again, if the section of healing from past hurt was skipped over you might want to go back and process it after you read this.

Have you ever tried to communicate with someone, and everything that you say offends them? Every question you asked is interpreted as a judgement against them? No matter how careful you are with your wording, how soft you are with your tone, or how much you wait for the right time to talk, they find a reason to be offended by what you say. Or maybe it is you that seems to be irritated by someone that has not really done anything to hurt you. May I suggest that the source of the reaction and behavior stems from past pain? Hurt affects our ability to properly communicate, because information gets filtered through experiences of trauma, memories of hurt, and feelings of disappointment. This destroys effective listening, creates arguments, and derails mutuality, because our interpretation of information is skewed by pain. You might have said, "Hello, how is your day?" to someone, and were ignored, frowned at, or given a defensive response. An individual that is dealing with hurt and anger interprets that simple question a lot differently from others. It was filtered through frustration so that controls their response. So if you did not have enough reason to heal from past hurt, you were just given more logic on the importance of it. Hurt affects our listening and sabotages all communication. Mutual listening takes a different set of ears than most. It takes being an individual that listens to build bridges with others in a society that has become accustomed to building walls.

A good listener makes others feel accepted and valued. If you want to build friendships, draw people to you and make them feel comfortable, become a good listener. Be a curious listener that shows interest in others. If most people believe that communication is one of the most important qualities to a good relationship, and listening is one of the most important aspects of communication, it would be a good idea to develop this skill as you prepare yourself to be in your next relationship.

TRUTH IN COMMUNICATION

There has never been a time in history where people have been so divided on what is true or false, what is propaganda or facts. The social media highlights that we choose to show of our lives have become reality, and truths that have stood the test of time and been passed down through generations have become questioned. With this, there has been a growing movement which supports the idea of individual truth. Meaning, I have the liberty to say what I want, do what I want, and believe how I want, and it is acceptable as long it is "my truth". This notion has been widely embraced by society. More people used to have a source where we got our truth from such as the Holy Bible, or for some, the Koran, or others that follow Torah. Truth today has been placed in our hands. Our feelings and emotions have become the basic sources of our truth.

Before I get to the importance of communicating in truth in order to have a mutuality mindset, I think that it is essential to discuss the importance of sharing that same truth in order to have a mutuality mindset. For us to think as one, we must operate from the same basic value system, we must govern our lives by similar rules, and we have to agree on the same fundamental beliefs, or having a mutuality mindset will forever be a struggle. I once heard someone say, "It is not enough that they respect your truths and beliefs, but they must share your truth and beliefs or it will not work". Some people might call this mutual truth, chemistry. A more spiritual person may label it as being equally yoked. However we decide to classify it we can be sure that communication flows better when we share the same fundamental truths about life, love, religion, behaviors, and consequences. So many times we attempt to create a bond with individuals that do not see the world as we do. They function with a different set of values, morals, and guidelines than we do. Then we wonder why communication is off, why we are constantly at odds when we talk, and why it seems like they do not listen to anything we say. That is because we are operating from two different set of truths, or should I say what we believe is true, because there is only one truth. The first key of communicating in truth is communicating to discover what each other's truth is with major things in life. If I believe that Jesus Christ is the Messiah, but my mate believes that He was just a righteous man, we do not share the same truth. That will eventually become a challenge.

Hopefully you understand the importance of sharing the same truth. Now let us talk about how crucial it is for that truth to be accurate. This means that we have to communicate with correctness, fairness, and wholeness. To have a mutuality mindset we must learn to communicate the full story, without omission of facts and experience. We cannot expect others to fill in the blanks then become frustrated because we are being misunderstood or misinterpreted. Half of the reason for misinterpretation and misunderstanding is the fact that we did not communicate the full truth. The other half might be that individual's refusal to accept the truth, but that is something that you as the speaker cannot change. Your job is to inform an individual, not conform an individual. I digress. To avoid misinterpretation and misunderstanding we cannot choose to withdraw and shut down. We cannot only communicate the side that makes us feel in control, or makes us look good. We cannot fail to communicate our mistakes, insecurities, fears, and vulnerabilities. That is not communicating in wholeness. When we fail to communicate in fullness we forfeit a perfect opportunity to build intimacy and trust. We miss the chance to initiate and display mutuality, and we leave things open for misinterpretation. I am willing to bet if the communication is about anything that is unpleasant or negatively affecting the relationship, the interpretation will not be in our favor. Honesty, fullness, and equality are the keys to communicating in truth, and they serve as great indicators that two people are ready for a healthy relationship.

TIMING AND TONE OF COMMUNICATION

In mutual communication we have to realize the importance of timing and tone. When addressing an issue, we have to consider the other person's readiness for discussion. We should consider the factors that can cause the communication to go positively or negatively. For example, if your mate just left a stressful day of work, just received bad news, or is sleepy, is that the best time to discuss important issues? Probably not. Timing is everything. A part of having a mutuality mindset is being so in tune with your mate that you can sense their moods, and you know the most effective time to communicate about serious issues with them. Some topics should not be brought up when you are mad, or when you are just relaxing, or in the middle of enjoyment. It is all about timing. The two of you should agree to communicate during a time that works well for both parties involved in order to get the best results. That will make the communication more productive, receptive and receivable.

Communication usually does not produce or destroy results based on what was said, but most of the time it is how it is said that makes all the difference. The tone of our communication means everything. It does not always matter how right we are in our position. If we communicate our correctness in the wrong tone we will cause a divide instead of mutuality and that truth will continue to fall on deaf ears. Using the appropriate tone means everything to some people, and developing a mutuality mindset means that we have to take out the time to learn how certain tones affect the person that we are trying to communicate with. If I come from a culture that speaks loudly, direct, and in your face with everything we say, but I am dating someone that is uncomfortable with that tone of communication because they come from an experience where yelling and loudness was the preamble to abuse, then my tone would be completely destructive to communication, and would probably kill any hope of getting on the same page.

In a mutuality mindset we seek to find a style of communication that works for the both of us. We develop the desire to take out time to find out what certain tones mean for the other person. We do not project our own meaning and interpretation on them. Loudness might mean excitement and enthusiasm to me, while loud talking can mean attention-seeking or anger to her. In mutuality we aim to figure that out with each other, then we make the proper adjustments to a tone that satisfies the both of us.

COMMUNICATE ON PRINCIPLE

We have heard the saying, "If you don't stand for something, you'll fall for anything". The 'something' that we stand on would be our principles. When we communicate we must make sure that it is based on principle. The foundation of our communication has to be built on what is right and not what feels good in the moment. We must communicate based on what is true and not just what is easier to do. We must communicate based on what is most beneficial and not what is most convenient. This takes us back to the importance of sharing the same principles, because if you do not share the same basic principles with the individual that you are dating or entertaining a relationship with, communication will break down before it even begins. Our principles govern our behaviors. They control what we will and will not do. Our principles set our priorities, and it is important that our principles are centered in truth and righteousness. Truth and righteousness are universal. Everyone may not agree with this, and it may hurt the feelings of some, but no one can say that it is wrong. This helps to create mutuality because the other person gets to know the ground that you stand on and vice versa. In certain situations you will find that you do not have wonder what they would think, and they do not have to ask your opinion, because they understand your principles. This truly helps communication and creates unity among two individuals. However if we do not communicate about principles through our speech as well as our actions, it will be a barrier to mutuality because we will appear as flaky and hypocritical. Our words will be considered shallow and our actions unpredictable. It is extremely hard for two people to work together if one of the individuals is constantly wavering in what they say they stand for.

COMMUNICATE IN LOVE

Communicating in love is more than speaking in a tender tone. It is more than using pet names, and it is not just saying the words "I love you". Learning to communicate in love is a major key to developing a mutuality mindset. Love is a universal language that unifies. It brings people together. It doesn't matter if you are black or white, heterosexual or homosexual, Christian or Muslim, when we speak in love it will diffuse any argument, disarm any attack, bring understanding to confusion, settle differences, and it will soften hatred. Speaking in love encompasses so many things, but the most important ingredient would be having our hearts in the right position. Our motives and intentions must be grounded in love. There has to be a genuine desire to want the best for others, help others, encourage others, and accept others. We must have an honest love for others.

If I could take a few words from the Bible as a way to describe love, you will see how hard it would be to not be in harmony with someone that communicated in love. 1 Corinthians 13 says that love is patient, kind, it does not boast; it is humble; it is not self-seeking, so it is selfless; and that love is not easily angered and does not keep record of wrongs, so love is peaceful and forgiving. It would be very hard for us not to be in harmony with someone else if we learned to communicate in love.

The core of building mutual communication does not start with the desire to be in a relationship. It does not begin with wanting companionship. It has to begin with a genuine goal to spread love. When we communicate in truth, the motive cannot be to prove someone wrong. The motive has to be to correct them in love. As we are listening attentively, the purpose cannot be to gather ammunition to fight back. The intent has to be to gain understanding so that we can love them better. During those times when we are angry, disappointed, or sad we still have to learn how to communicate with love. In fact, that is when we should increase our love-filled communication, because during times of anger and frustration we can say things that can hurt others and destroy a relationship because we spoke from the wrong emotion. When we decide to communicate in love we are deciding to do all of the things that we previously discussed: communicate using the right tone, communicate using the right timing, communicate using the right wording, and we communicate while standing on the right principles. Our speech is purposeful and that purpose is finding mutuality, peace, and harmony. In order to be ready for a relationship we must practice these things. We have to begin communicating in love with others so that when we do meet the person that we want to be in a committed relationship with we have already prepared ourselves.

Conclusion

Growth starts internally, and the only person that we can change is ourselves. As the saying goes, "We must be the change that we want to see." If we want love, we must become loving. If we want peace, we must become peaceful. If we want to be understood, we must become understanding. Being ready for a relationship requires us to work on ourselves. Having that man in the mirror moment, and dealing with the issues that make us unprepared. We have to stop looking outside of ourselves for the answers to, "Why we cannot find a good mate?"; "Why do our relationships always end the same?"; or "Why we seem to attract the same type of person?" We have to begin to look at the common dominator in all of these questions; then we will find the answer. The truth is, we can be our worst enemy at times. We are the ones who stop ourselves from getting what we want out of life, and the whole purpose of this book is to show you that we have the power to change that by taking control of the way we live and exist in this world. We have the power to heal from what has been hurting us. We are in control of gaining that self-knowledge and self-awareness so that we truly know who we are as a person. It is up to us to develop our spiritual life and gain fulfillment from God so we are no longer looking for fulfillment in others, or only take from others, but we become a giver. We have the freedom to let others into our world so that we can have the love and life we desire.

The four keys outlined throughout the book: healing from past hurt, knowing thine self, knowing God, and developing a mutuality mindset, are a great place to start on our road toward relationship readiness. As we travel this journey we may discover more principles. We should realize that we never stop growing, and we never stop adjusting and learning. Even when we enter into a relationship, there will be more growing to do. Internal growth does not stop with these four steps, but if you are having challenges with figuring out where to start, allow this book to be the springboard that helps you dive into the journey toward relationship readiness. Be blessed.

www.ingramcontent.com/pod-product-compliance
Lightning Source LLC
Chambersburg PA
CBHW020850090426
42736CB00008B/311